Creative Kids
Complete Photo Guide to

Bead Crafts

First published in the United States of America by
Creative Publishing international, a division of
Quarto Publishing Group USA Inc.
400 First Avenue North
Suite 400
Minneapolis, MN 55401
1-800-328-3895
www.creativepub.com
Visit www.Craftside.net for a behind-the-scenes peek at our
crafty world!

ISBN: 978-1-58923-822-0

Library of Congress Cataloging-in-Publication Data available

Copy Editor: Jennifer Kushnier
Design and Layout: Laura McFadden
Bead illustrations: Amy Kopperude
Illustrations of Kids: iStock
Photographs: Tony Hamel, Amy Kopperude,
Shutterstock (p.6)
Printed in USA

Creative Kids

Complete
Photo Guide to
Bead
Crafts

Amy Kopperude

**Creative Publishing
international**
www.creativepub.com

contents

Introduction

When I first began playing with beads as a child, I had a cardboard box filled with pipe cleaners, yarn, plastic pony beads, buttons, and more. I liked to experiment, but I didn't have anything near the range of supplies that are available today for kids' bead crafts. Walk into any craft store, and the aisles are not only packed with beading and stringing varieties, but also cover an experience level ranging from novice to artist. You can be any age, any experience level, with any range of ideas for projects and be absolutely stellar at beading, if only you have an imagination (and sometimes, patience). That's all it takes!

If you can dream, then the gamut of bead crafting is endless. You can start out with large-hole beads like pony beads and work your way toward more intricate glass beads. Some beads, like fusible beads, are rarely strung, but instead melted together to make works of art like drink coasters or window decorations. You can even make your own beads, and *Creative Kids Complete Photo Guide to Bead Crafts* will show you how to do that, too!

If you're just starting out with bead crafts, then stringing beads onto pipe cleaners or jelly cord—and using your fingers to bend, loop, and tie—will be much easier than learning to manipulate various wire gauges with round- and flat-nose pliers. But the more you experiment with new techniques and the more you practice, the better you will get—and the better your final work will be.

Don't let fancy tools and supplies scare you. Many times, you can substitute one tool or supply for another with a little ingenuity. This book will also show you how to use tools ranging from simple household items like scissors and cylinder-shape dowels and bottles to more complex bead craft–specific pliers and snips. In addition, these pages will teach you how to tie parachute cord and jute twine using macramé techniques, how to weave beads onto string by following a pattern, how to make projects ranging from jewelry and accessories to sculptural pieces and decorations, and much more.

The projects in *Creative Kids Complete Photo Guide to Bead Crafts* are designed for both boys and girls at a variety of skill levels, so there's something for everyone. Parents and kids can create together, or parents can be on standby to help with safety steps like ironing or intricate steps like finishing touches. So prepare yourself for hours of creative fun, and let's get started!

basics

Before you get started making the projects in this book, practice making your own beads, charms, and pendants with the nine mini-projects in this section, and then take some time to get familiar with all of the different types of materials and tools used for beadwork. Finally, get acquainted with some of the techniques you'll be using for the fifteen projects in the last section of the book.

All about Beads, Charms, and Pendants

You will be amazed by what you can create with so many different kinds of beads, especially when you cannot only purchase them from a craft store, but also make them in your own home. Most craft stores sell variety packs of colorful plastic shape (A) and pony (B) beads. These are excellent for starting out. In addition to being colorful, some of the beads for children are metallic (C), or they can be linked together, as is the case with tri-shape and sunburst beads (D). Fusible beads (E) are placed on a peg board in a pattern and then heated with an iron until they melt together, but they can also

be used for beading. If you want to work with more natural beads, craft stores also sell wooden and nature-tone beads (F). Glass beads (G) are great for projects like the Seashell Wind Chimes on page 61, because of their detail and sophistication. Seed beads (H), which are used for the daisy chain bookmark project on page 120, can also be used by experienced and patient crafters for embroidery work. This is only the beginning of what you'll find when you start looking for beads. Specialty shops carry beads made from recycled materials and even mood beads!

Make Your Own Beads

If you like to think outside the box or if you have a lot of resources but not the means to buy beads, then making your own beads is the ticket to a one-of-a-kind finished project. Making your own beads requires some patience and creativity, but people will "ooh" and "aah" when they see what you made.

Totally Tubular Beads

Perhaps the easiest "bead" to make yourself is also one right under your nose! Instead of throwing away a drinking or stirring straw, cut it into segments to use as beads. You can cut the pieces short or long. You can even cut notches or a fringe into them with fine-point scissors like embroidery scissors. Start saving colorful and striped straws for bright and cheery creations. Restaurants and coffee shops sometimes carry thin stirring straws. Colorful paper straws can be purchased online or at party-supply and craft stores.

Dyed Pasta Beads

Many types of pasta—rigatoni, macaroni, penne, wagon wheels, and small stars and circles—are easy to thread onto beading string because they already have holes. To create colorful pasta beads, follow the simple directions on page 13.

You Will Need

- 1 tablespoon (15 ml) rubbing alcohol
- 1 teaspoon (5 ml) gel food coloring
- 1-gallon (3.8 L) plastic resealable bag (one for each color)
- 2 cups (about 200 g) pasta
- parchment paper

Directions

1. Put 1 tablespoon (15 ml) rubbing alcohol and 1 teaspoon (5 ml) gel food coloring in the resealable bag and squish together.

2. Add 2 cups pasta to the bag and seal shut. Gently mix the pasta around in the bag so that it is evenly coated with food coloring. Allow to sit for one hour.

3. Place parchment paper on a clean countertop or table. Gently pour the colored pasta onto the parchment paper, keeping the colors separate. Allow to dry completely for several hours before using.

Paper Beads

Long before a variety of beads could be purchased at craft stores, people made beads from paper. The following directions are for a simple oval bead, but the Internet is a great source for more challenging and detailed paper-bead templates.

You Will Need

- paper (origami paper, a page from a magazine, or a colorful road map)

- ruler

- pencil

- scissors

- paintbrush

- round toothpicks (one for each bead)

- clear-drying craft glue or clear sealer/finisher

Directions

1 The thickness of each bead depends on the length and width of each paper strip. To make oval tube beads, use the ruler to measure rectangular strips of paper that are ½" × 11" (1.5 cm × 28 cm). Mark the measurements with a pencil. (Hint: Scrapbook paper sheets often measure 11" [28 cm] long, so you would have to measure only the strip widths.) Do this step for the number of beads you wish to make.

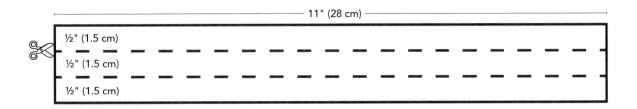

11" (28 cm)

½" (1.5 cm)
½" (1.5 cm)
½" (1.5 cm)

(continued)

2 Mark the middle point of one end of each rectangular piece (A). Lay the ruler starting at the mark you just made and finishing at the top corner of the opposite end of the strip of paper. Draw a line to connect the points (B). Repeat this with the ruler starting at the bottom corner of the opposite end and finishing at the middle mark (C). You will have created what looks like a long triangle.

A

B

C

3 Use the scissors to cut out the triangular strips.

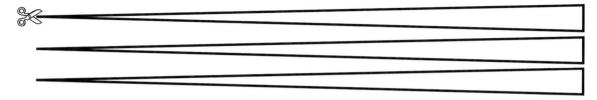

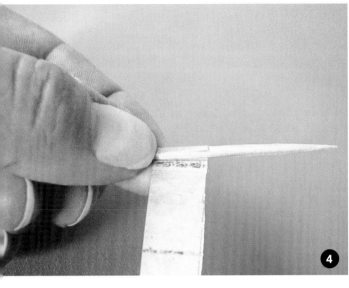

4 Starting with the wide edge of each paper strip, wrap the paper strip tightly and uniformly around a toothpick so that the design of the paper is on the outside.

5 When you reach the end of the paper, apply a dab of craft glue to the inside of the paper point and press the point against the bead.

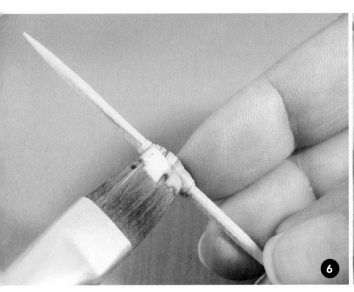

6 Use the paintbrush to apply a coat of glue (or other clear sealer/finisher) to the outside of the bead.

7 Allow to dry before removing the bead from the toothpick.

Duct Tape Beads

Making duct tape beads is very similar to making paper beads. Duct tape is thicker and makes a chunkier bead. Because the tape is already sticky, the bead requires no glue or sealer to keep it from unraveling. Duct tape beads are great for small fingers and kids who are just getting started with beading, as long as an adult is present to cut or assist with cutting the strips. If you don't have a cutting mat or rotary cutter, you can also use a clean cutting surface and a craft knife.

You Will Need

- 9" (23 cm) of duct tape
- drinking straw with preferred hole diameter for beading
- cutting mat
- straight edge
- rotary cutter

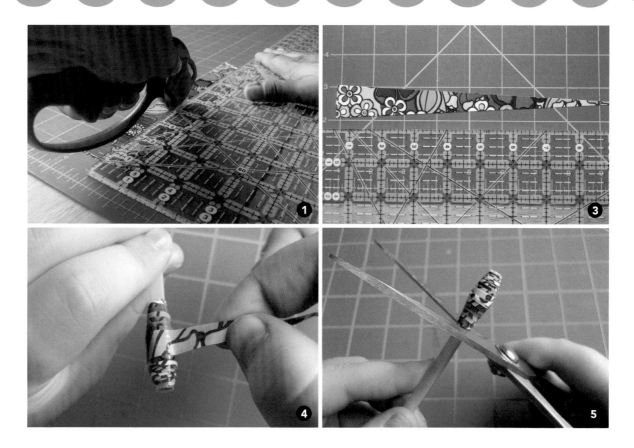

Directions

1 Place a 9" (23 cm) strip of duct tape on the cutting mat, keeping it lined up with a measurement rule.

2 Using a straight edge and a rotary cutter, cut the duct tape strip in half lengthwise.

3 Cut each half strip into a long triangle, cutting from the outer corners of one end to the center of the other end. Don't discard the long thin triangles that remain on each side.

4 Pull up the center triangular strip of tape from the cutting mat. Stick the wide end to the straw, and begin to wind the tape against the straw, keeping the tapered edges centered as you wind. Use the long thin side triangles to make smaller beads. Or, wrap two of them with the straight outer edges right next to each other, to make a bead the same size as the center triangle bead.

5 Cut the excess straw from each end of the bead.

Polymer Clay Beads

Working with polymer can be a lot of fun, especially since the clay requires heat to harden so your project won't dry out while you're working on it. To make your own beads, you will need to first knead the clay with your hands so that it becomes pliable. Simply roll it between your fingers to warm it up. Then, here are three different beginner beads that you can make with it. Just before baking these beads, push them onto a piece of heavy-gauge wire (thicker wire will make a larger hole) and bake them with the wire in place. Remove the wire when the bead has cooled. Follow the manufacturer's instructions for baking the clay in the oven.

You Will Need

- polymer clay in various colors
- rolling pin
- waxed paper
- straight edge
- craft knife

Round Polka-Dot Beads

Roll a pea-size piece of clay in the palm of your hand until you have made a ball. Choose a different color(s) of clay and roll breadcrumb-size amounts between two fingers. Make several of these and push them into the original ball of clay in various places. Roll the ball in the palm of your hand again to reform it into a more spherical shape.

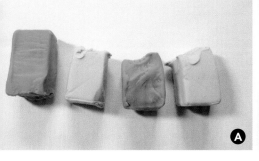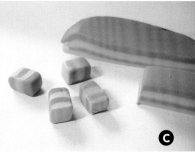

Striped Cube Beads

Use one scored strip of two different colors of polymer clay for this bead. Divide each strip in half the short way (A), and use a rolling pin to roll each of them onto a piece of waxed paper until they are approximately ¼" (6 mm) thick. Stack the colors, every other one, so that you have four slabs of clay in layers (B). Gently use a rolling pin to fuse them together. Then, use a straight edge, such as a plastic gift card or craft knife, to trim the edges off the clay and divide the slab into cubed sections (C).

Candy Stick Beads

Use half of one scored strip of two different colors of polymer clay for this bead. Roll each color against a flat, clean surface with your hand to form a long uniform worm about ¼" (6 mm) thick (A). Twist the two colors together (B), and then gently roll the "worm" against your work surface again to fuse the colors (C). Use a craft knife to cut the twisted cane into segments (D).

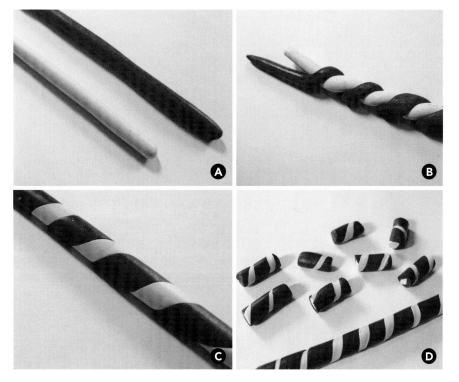

Make Your Own Charms and Pendants

Charms and pendants are often the focal design of any piece of jewelry, and you can even collect charms to make a personalized charm bracelet. Although many charms and pendants can be purchased to add to a piece of jewelry (or some other project), you might not find the right charm for your project and want to make your own instead. So let's explore some possibilities for creating your own charms and pendants.

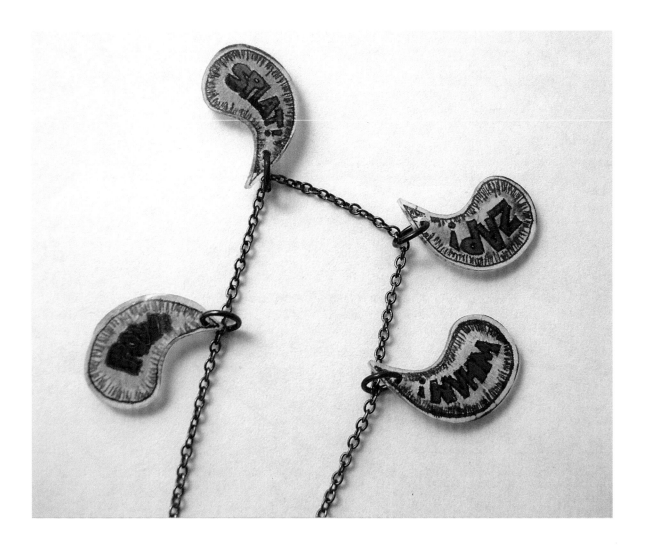

You Will Need

- frosted shrinkable plastic sheet

- fine-point permanent markers in a variety of colors

- ¼" (6 mm) hole paper punch

- scissors, craft knife, or large-shape paper punch

Shrinkable Plastic Charms

Shrinkable plastic sheets come in various colors. Use white or transparent sheets for drawing images with permanent markers. Use colored shrinkable plastic to make shapes using scissors or shaped paper punches.

Directions

1 Follow the manufacturer's instructions for drawing and coloring an image onto the rough side of the shrinkable plastic. Draw an image three times the intended size because it will shrink down to one-third of the original size. (If using a large-shape paper punch, cut out the shape first. Then, draw and color the image onto the shape.)

2 Use the scissors to cut out the colored image (if not using a large-shape paper punch). For detailed cutting, a craft knife may work better.

3 Use the hole paper punch to create the hole for the finished piece.

4 Follow the manufacturer's instructions for baking the plastic piece in the oven. After the pendant has cooled, a jump ring can be added to the hole to hang it from a necklace (see page 46 for instructions).

Glass Marble Charms

Glass decorating gems look like round, flattened marbles and are used to fill vases and candle holders. They come in many colors and designs, but to make them into charms using photos or clip art, look for high-quality transparent gems (no luster) that have no blemishes on the flat side. A ripple in the glass will make it difficult to see the image that you apply to the back.

You Will Need

- 1 transparent glass decorating gem
- color-printed image or patterned paper cut into a ⅝" (1.5 cm)-diameter circle
- 1 pea-size amount of baking clay
- clear-drying craft glue
- straight edge
- 1 small eye screw
- sheet of aluminum foil

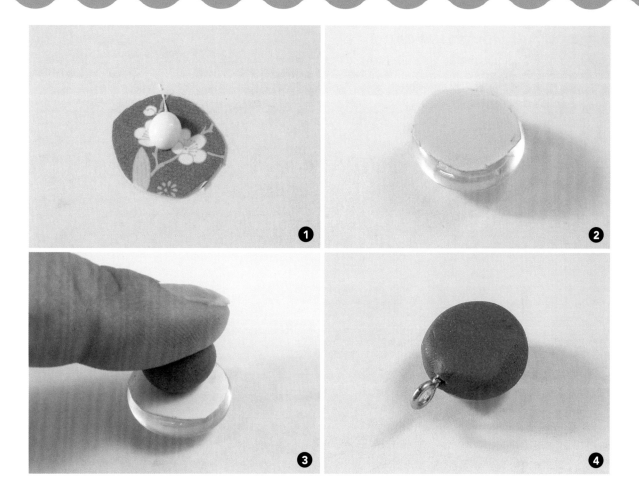

Directions

1 Cut out the color-printed image or piece of patterned paper. Apply a thin layer of craft glue over the surface of the image.

2 Press the image against the flat size of the glass marble. Allow to dry until the image is clearly visible through the glass marble.

3 Press the pea-size amount of baking clay against the back of the marble over the paper image and gently maneuver it until it covers the paper and touches the sides of the marble. Use a straight edge, such as a plastic gift card, to trim excess clay from the outside edge, and use a smooth surface (a table top, the surface of your fingernail) to flatten out any ripples in the clay.

4 Push the eye screw into the clay at the top of the charm. Shape the clay around the eye screw as needed so that just the eye is showing.

5 Place the charm, clay side down, on a sheet of aluminum foil and follow the manufacturer's instructions for baking the piece in the oven. Remove from the oven and allow to cool.

Pressed Salt Dough Pendants

Salt dough is the perfect medium for more rustic creations. When salt dough bakes, the potential exists for minor cracks and bumps to form, which can add character to a piece. The salt dough recipe can also be used to make beads if a more natural look is preferred.

You Will Need

- 2 cups (250 g) all-purpose flour (do not use self-rising flour)
- 1 cup (288 g) table salt
- 1 cup (235 ml) water
- bowl
- mug or glass
- toothpick or skewer
- baking sheet or sheet of aluminum foil
- paintbrush
- clear sealer/finisher
- *Optional:* metal- or clay-stamping tools or leather-tooling stamps; acrylic paint

Directions

1 Preheat the oven to 250°F (121°C).

2 Mix the flour and salt together in the bowl, and then add the water. Use a spoon or your hands to mix the ingredients together until a dough forms. The dough should not be sticky.

3 Knead the dough for several minutes until it is smooth and firm.

(continued)

4 Roll a marble-size amount of dough between your hands until a ball is formed. Use the bottom of a mug or glass to flatten the round ball.

5 Consider using stamping tools or leather-tooling stamps to personalize the pendant with name initials or to add texture and depth (A). Don't forget to poke a hole into the top of the pendant with a toothpick or skewer (B).

6 Place the pendant onto a baking sheet or piece of aluminum foil and put it in the oven for approximately two hours.

7 Remove the pendant, and allow it to cool. Then, paint the pendant, if desired, and apply a clear sealer/finisher to protect the paint and to prevent the salt dough from softening over time due to humidity. Store any unused dough in an airtight container in the refrigerator for up to five days.

Decoupage Pendants

Game pieces such as Scrabble® letter tiles and dominos—and even bottle caps—have become popular for jewelry making, and there are a number of ways to design them as pendants. Decoupage whimsical images or old family photos onto a game piece, or paint a miniature masterpiece. Add glitter or gems, or tie a fabric scrap to the bail. Glue-on bails can be purchased through most craft outlets and attach easily to the flat backing of these game pieces.

You Will Need

- Scrabble® letter tile or domino tile

- decoupage paper or old photo

- scissors

- clear-finishing decoupage medium

- paintbrush

- jewelry glue

- 1 metal bail

- *Optional:* fabric scraps, ribbon, letter beads, glitter, gems

Directions

1 Cut out images and arrange them on the game piece. Follow the manufacturer's directions for applying a decoupage medium using a paint-brush to adhere the images. Coat the entire surface of the decoupaged game piece with the medium. When dry, trim any excess from edges.

2 Glue on dimensional objects like letter beads, gems, or glitter. To add glitz to the game piece, brush glue around the outside edges and dip the edges into the glitter. Allow to dry completely.

3 When the entire pendant is dry, apply the metal bail to the top back of the pendant with jewelry glue. Allow several hours to dry.

Create with Nonbeads

Experimentation with making beads, charms, and pendants often leads to the realization that many small objects, if they have a hole or opening, are good for beading. Buttons are great for macramé. Metal keys can be painted. Nuts and washers can be strung up in a graduated fashion for a unique look. Acorns and other nuts and seeds can be made into beads if an adult uses a rotary tool with a very small drill bit to create a hole. Old plastic gift cards can be cut up and hole punched to be made into earrings. Using a threaded needle, pom-poms can be strung as beads, too. Sequins are ready-made spacers to put between other beads for more shine.

Materials and Tools

This picture glossary of materials and tools will guide you in understanding what various beadwork items look like and how they are used. The "You Will Need" list of each project includes the materials and tools that are described in more detail here. Refer to this glossary to answer any questions about beading materials.

Wire

Wire comes in various gauges and colors for a variety of projects including beading and wire wrapping. Heavy gauges are more difficult to manipulate and better for wire wrapping than beading because many beads won't fit over the thicker wire. Soft gauge wire is better for more intricate work and for threading beads, but will break if it is manipulated too much.

Coated Wire

Coated wire (e.g., telephone wire) is used to make the Cootie Bug Study Buddy on page 80. Coated wire can be purchased new from a hardware store or as recycled material online. The striped and colorful wire is very easy for small hands to manipulate without tools and is great for simple projects that require large-hole beads.

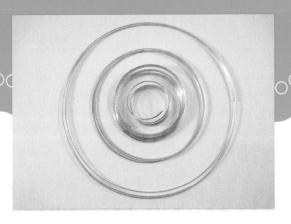

Colored Copper Wire

Copper wire is sold in a variety of colors and gauges. The gauge is important depending on the size of the holes in the beads that are being used for a project. The hard gauges (e.g., typically lower than 22 gauge) require beads with bigger holes and are often more difficult to bend. The soft gauges (e.g., 24, 26, 28) are very easy to bend and often more fragile. Colored copper wire is used to make the Fairy Bubble Wand on page 54, the Button Ring on page 96, and the Crystal Night-Light Shade on page 110.

Memory Wire

Memory wire is sold in coiled sizes and is used to make preformed necklaces, bracelets, and rings. The circular shape of the wire is resistant to bending, so memory wire is preferred for wrapped jewelry such as the Twirly Whirly Watch Bracelet on page 92.

Strings 'n Things

Beads can be threaded onto many different types of string and cord. Choosing the right fiber for bead threading is essential for the final outcome of a project. Whereas some fibers like jute and nylon are durable; other "fibers"—like jelly cord and pipe cleaners—have elasticity for making bracelets or will bend and conform nicely for shaped projects. Each project identifies exactly what you will need.

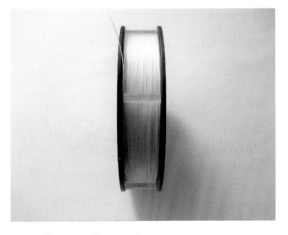

Beading Thread

Nylon beading thread and other fiber threads are best for projects with closely woven beaded rows because the thread responds well to any curves in the beaded strand and produces a nice drape. The Daisy Chain Bookmark on page 120 requires a soft, pliable beading thread to retain the shape and tension of the flowers.

(continued)

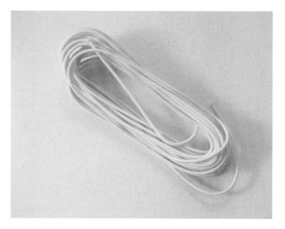

Elastic Cord

Elastic cord is a stretchy cord used for large-hole beads. It can be purchased in a variety of colors and metallics, as well as weights. It works well for bracelets because it can be beaded, tied in a knot, and then stretched to get it on and off the wrist without having to open any kind of clasp.

Jute Twine

Jute is a strong natural fiber that works well for tying projects like macramé and friendship bracelets, especially if a rugged look is preferred. The macramé skater cuff on page 114 is made with jute.

Jelly Cord (Stretchy Cord)

Jelly cord, also called stretchy cord, is elastic in nature but is a strong, stretchy, transparent material that hides well in beading projects, like the Beach Comber Flip-Flops on page 106. Jelly cord is also used to attach the hair combs to the tiara on page 100 because it is invisible against the pipe cleaner.

Parachute Cord

Parachute cord is a woven nylon cord with some elasticity that comes in sizes that refer to the cord's breaking strength (such as "550 pounds"). The core of the cord is typically made up of several triple-woven strands of yarn surrounded by the nylon sheath. Parachute cord is popular for bulky macramé projects with strong plastic clasps, like the utility fob on page 86.

Pipe Cleaners

Craft pipe cleaners are soft colorful fibers within twisted strands of wire that are easily pliable for making fuzzy creations. They are sold in a variety of colors, sizes, and even shapes. Bump pipe cleaners, for instance, look wavy and are used to support the eye beads in the Cootie Bug Study Buddy project on page 80.

Yarn

Synthetic yarn is affordable and great for projects for young children. For bead crafts, it can be crocheted or woven and used for stringing beads together.

Bits 'n Pieces

The bits and pieces you will need for the projects in this book are what many beadwork enthusiasts refer to as "findings." These are the small objects used for linking and attaching beads, thread, and wire.

Bail

A bail is a small piece of looped metal for attaching a pendant to a chain. Some bails have a hook on one end and a loop on the other, whereas other bails have an enclosed loop with a flat piece of metal to glue to a pendant. The enclosed loop bail is used to make the decoupage pendant described on page 30.

(continued)

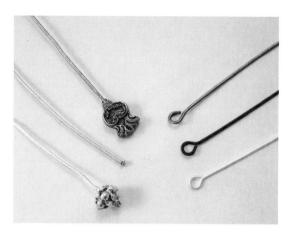

Charm Pin

A charm pin has metal rings for hanging beads and charms, but even a large safety pin can be beaded with charms and beads to make the Friendship Charm Pin on page 66.

Head Pin or Eye Pin

A head pin is a straight piece of wire with a flat, round, or ornamental end to keep beads from sliding off. An eye pin has one looped end instead of a flat end. The Seasonal Zipper Pulls on pages 72 and 73 use head pins.

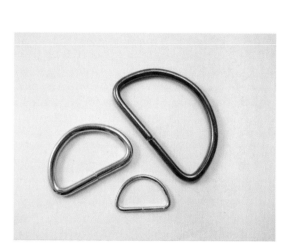

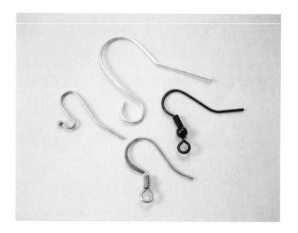

D-Ring

A D-ring is a D-shaped metal ring that comes in a variety of sizes. The straight side of the D-ring is usually attached to a fabric strip, such as at the end of a belt or dog leash. The School Spirit Utility Fob on page 86 is woven onto a swivel hook ring that has a D-ring so that it can be attached to keys, a belt loop, or a bag.

Ear Wire

An ear wire is the piece of an earring that goes into a pierced ear hole. It is shaped like an upside-down U and has a loop at one end for attaching a beaded creation, such as in the fusible bead Marigold Earrings project on page 52.

Jump/Split Ring

A jump ring is a looped piece of wire used to connect beaded strands. Jump rings are used to connect the hook or ear wires to the fusible bead objects in the projects on pages 51–52. Split rings are similar to jump rings but the wires overlap.

Lobster Clasp

A lobster clasp is a hook fastener with a small lever for opening and closing the hook to attach to a jump ring, like at the end of a necklace chain. It is used for making friendship charms to attach to a pin (see Friendship Charm Pin project on page 66).

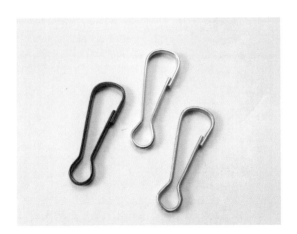

Metal Hook

A metal hook is opened by pushing against the inner part of the hook to separate it from the arch of the hook. The base of the hook can be beaded or used to attach a small object like the snowman and dragonfly zipper pulls on pages 72–73.

Plastic Hook

A plastic hook is larger than a metal hook and easier to open and close. It is used for the fusible bead back-pack clip projects on page 51.

Tools

You can't make projects with beads without some basic tools for cutting and shaping string and wire. In addition, you'll need tools from around the house like glue or even an iron and an oven to adhere pieces together.

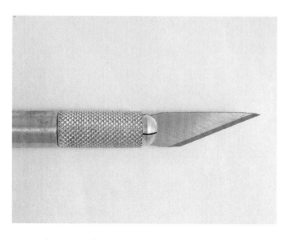

Craft Knife

A craft knife is a small utility knife used for precision cutting. The angled razor blade can be exchanged for a new blade when it becomes dull. A craft knife is used to cut the fusible beads to cover the ear bud wires in the project on page 53 and should be used only by an adult or a young adult under careful supervision.

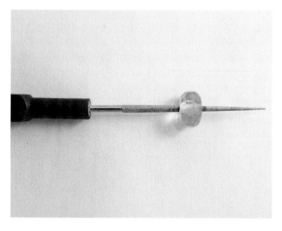

Bead Reamer

A bead reamer is a hand-held tool used to remove obstructions from a bead hole. The reamer is placed inside the hole and twisted back and forth. This tool is handy for the Seashell Wind Chimes on page 58.

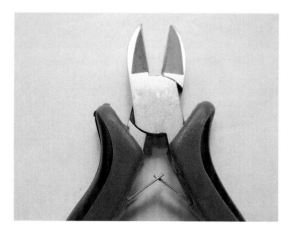

Cutters

Jewelry wire cutters have blades with different angles for different purposes. In general, however, any wire cutters can be used for the projects in this book. Many of the projects require cutting some type of wire, whether it be coated telephone wire, pipe cleaners, or memory wire.

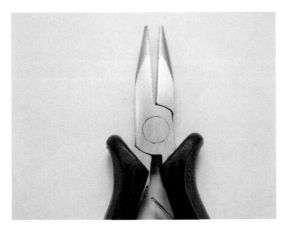

Flat-Nose Pliers

Flat-nose pliers are useful for bending wire at right angles and tightening/flattening coiled wire.

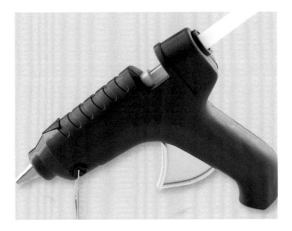

Glue Gun

A crafter's hot glue gun is an electrical tool used to fuse materials together. A cylindrical glue stick (which can be purchased in a package of multiples) is pushed through a chamber at the back of the tool, and hot, melted glue comes out of the nozzle when the trigger is squeezed. A glue gun typically has a metal easel for setting up the tool while it's heating or not in use, and care should be taken not to touch the nozzle or the melted glue while the tool is plugged in. A hot glue gun is used to fuse the white feather boa trim to the night light in the project on page 110.

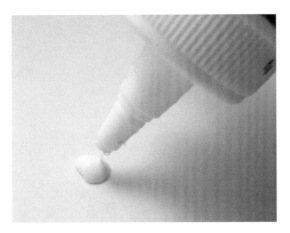

Glue

The projects in this book use a strong craft glue such as Aleene's Tacky Glue. Jewelry glues that require room ventilation or that cannot come into contact with skin are neither necessary nor recommended for the projects in this book.

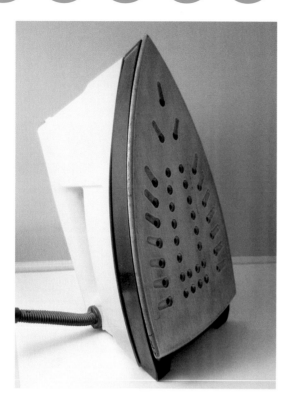

Paper Punch

A hole paper punch and shape paper punch can be used for materials slightly heavier than paper, such as shrinkable plastic.

Iron

An iron is used to melt together the fusible beads for the projects on pages 50–52 and should be used only by an adult or young adult under close adult supervision.

Oven

An oven is required for baking the clay and shrinkable plastic mini-projects. Only an adult or young adult under supervision should use an oven for the mini-projects.

Rotary Tool

A battery-powered rotary tool has multiple uses. Various bits can be purchased to drill, sand, bore holes through, cut, and create precision shaping of wood and other surfaces. A rotary tool should be used by an adult to drill holes in seashells for the Seashell Wind Chimes project on page 58.

Rotary Cutter

A rotary cutter is most often used in quilting to cut straight lines along a straight edge. A cutting mat is placed underneath the rotary cutter for a smooth, measured cut.

Scissors

Scissors can be used to cut a multitude of materials: paper, fiber, plastic, even soft-gauge wire. In lieu of wire cutters, scissors can be used for some of the projects in this book. Scissors are an easy cutting instrument for young children and often are the preferred method of cutting.

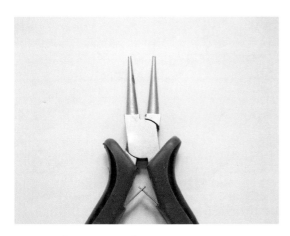

Round-Nose Pliers

Round-nose pliers are used to bend wire into loops and spirals. Refer to the illustrations on page 45 to learn how to use round-nose pliers. A pencil or dowel can also be used for more pliable wire, like telephone wire, especially for younger children who may have difficulty holding and using the round-nose pliers.

Techniques

Once you understand the materials and tools necessary for the projects in this book, you can learn exactly how to use some of them by applying techniques such as threading beads, macramé tying, and manipulating wire into loops and spirals with different pliers.

Threading Beads

There are many different gauges of wire, as well as various widths and types of stringing material, so the most important guideline to keep in mind when threading beads is whether the diameter of the bead's hole is big enough for the type of wire, thread, or other material you are using.

Once the correct beads and stringing material have been determined, simply thread the beads onto the stringing material. There may be times when a needle is necessary—for instance, if a bead's hole is rough or slightly obstructed, as may be the case with handmade glass beads.

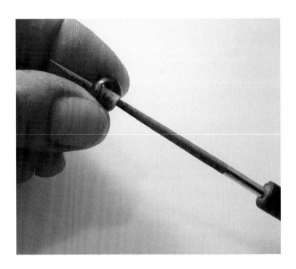

If a bead's hole has an obstruction, use a bead reamer to smooth it away.

Tying Macramé

Macramé is both functional and pretty. It has often been associated with plant hangers and hammocks. Even friendship bracelets made with embroidery floss or necklaces made with jute twine use macramé techniques. Macramé is simply a fancy way of tying and knotting string or fiber, and beads are a popular way to beautify a macramé jewelry project. Macramé knotting is required for the parachute cord utility fob on page 86 and the jute skater cuff on page 114.

Each macramé project starts with several strings that are secured at one end, which means that the strings are tied together or attached to an object like a key ring or D-ring.

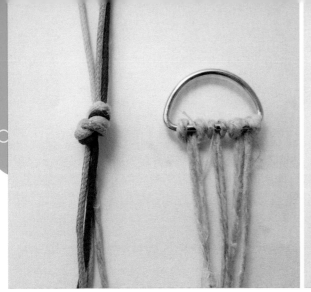

Macramé tying is easiest if you pin the project to a surface so that tying the strings can be done both efficiently and uniformly. It's important to secure each knot so that the pattern you are following results in a creation that has a consistent look. When I was a teen and making a lot of friendship bracelets for my friends, I pinned the knotted threads to the corner of a bed pillow and then laid the strings across the pillow so I could easily see what I was working on. Then, if I didn't finish a bracelet right away, I could set the pillow aside and work on the bracelet later.

Two popular macramé techniques for working with embroidery floss and jute twine are illustrated next. These techniques can be used for necklaces, bracelets, lanyards, and more. When you create the utility fob and skater cuff in this book, you will probably discover the similarities across projects.

Embroidery Floss

Using four (or more) strands of embroidery floss (approximately 1½ yards [1½ meters] of each strand), start with the strands all knotted at one end. Begin each row from left to right, tying the first strand to the second strand and so forth. Lay the first strand over the second strand in a "number 4"–shaped loop, folding strand 1 under strand 2 and bringing it up through the center of the "number 4" (A). While holding down strand 2, gently pull strand 1 up to the original knot of four strands to create row 1, column 1 of the bracelet (B). Continue to tie strand 1 to strand 3, then strand 4, and so on in the same manner until you reach the end of the row (C and D). Lay strand 1 with the other strands before starting a new row (E). Begin the new row with strand 2 looping around strand 3, then strand 4, and so on. This pattern will create a diagonal stripe. To create thicker stripes, make two loops instead of one loop on each strand. To make a diamond pattern, start with at least 6 strands of embroidery floss and work from each outer edge into the center, tying each row in the center, then working from the center back to each outer edge.

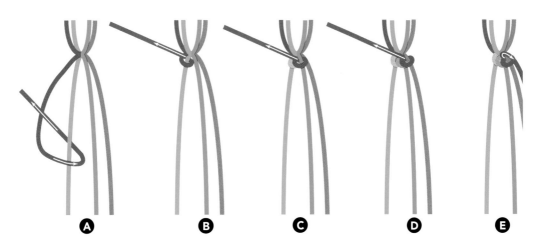

(A)　　　(B)　　　(C)　　　(D)　　　(E)

Jute Twine

Jute is thicker than embroidery floss, so using the embroidery floss technique with this fiber will result in a thicker bracelet using less length. A technique for working with jute requires fewer motions but slightly more finesse. Use four strands of jute, as with the previous example for an embroidery floss friendship bracelet, and make sure that two of the strands are about half the length longer than the other two strands. Tie the four strands together at one end, and place the longer strands to the outside.

Again, use the "number 4" looping technique, but this time work strand 1 over both strands 2 and 3. Then, use a backward "number 4" looping technique with strand 4, being sure to go over strand 1, behind strands 3 and 2, and up through the "number 4" hole created by strand 1 (A). Doing your best to hold down the middle two strands, pull strands 1 and 4 up against your original knot of four strands. As you pull these strands to secure them, notice the pretzel shape of the knot (B).

For the next row, run strand 1 *behind* strands 2 and 3, and run strand 4 (backwards) *over* strands 3 and 2. Basically, treat strand 1 as strand 4 from the previous row and strand 4 as strand 1 from the previous row (C). Continue to alternate the pattern for rows 1 and 2 until you reach the desired length for your project.

Be creative with beads by adding them either to the two center strands or to either strand 1 or 4 right before you secure the pretzel knot.

These macramé projects can be finished the way they were started—with a knot that secures all four strands. See also the utility fob and skater cuff projects for different ideas for starting and finishing a macramé knotting project.

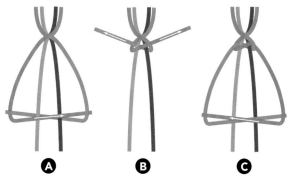

Working with Wire

So many jewelry findings are made with wire: head and eye pins, jump rings, ear wires, chain, and more. Some findings can be made with jewelry tools and a handful of techniques. A few of those techniques are described here.

Making Loops and Spirals

Use a pair of round-nose pliers to grip the end of a piece of wire (A), preferably a medium gauge that won't bend too easily but also won't be so thick as to be difficult to work with (22- to 24-gauge should work best). Rotate the pliers, wrapping the wire one full turn around one jaw of the pliers (B). When you have reached one rotation, you have a **loop** for one jump ring. Remove the loop and snip off the excess wire using wire cutters. To make several jump rings, wrap the wire around the jaw of the pliers several times in a tight **spiral** (C). Then remove the spiral and cut through one side (all rows of spiraled wire) to make several jump rings (D). The round-nose pliers are cone shaped, so you can make many different sizes of loops and spirals.

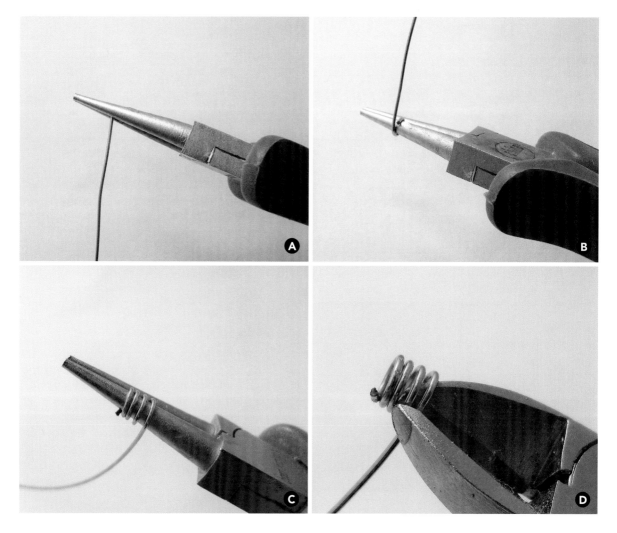

Making Coils

To make a **coil**, grip the wire just as you did for creating a loop and wrap the wire around the very tip of the round-nose pliers so that you have the smallest curve possible (A, B). Once you have a sharp curve in the wire, use a pair of flat-nose pliers to continue to curve your long piece of wire around the sharp curve that you started with. You will need to use your free hand to help bend the wire into a coil (C). The flat-nose pliers will keep the coil flat and together for a uniform look.

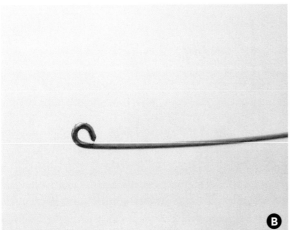

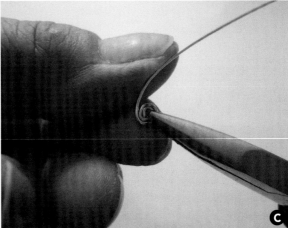

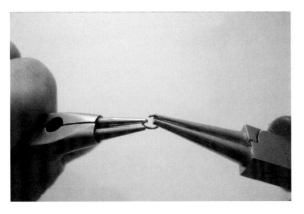

Opening and Closing a Jump Ring

Use two pairs of flat-nose (or other) pliers to grip each side of a jump ring near the opening. Then, bring one hand toward you and the other hand away from you at the same time. Never pull the ring out to the sides because it weakens the wire and distorts the ring. Close the jump ring the same way it was opened.

Twisting Wire Together

Holding two high-gauge (soft) wires together at the ends, use both hands to twist the wires together in the same manner that you would use to close a twist tie on a loaf of bread. Twist to the preferred length.

If you want to add beads to the twisted strand, separate the wires when you have reached a preferred length (A), thread a bead onto just one wire (B), then continue twisting the strands together until you reach the next preferred length (C). Continue threading beads and twisting the wires until the strand is the length you need for your project.

A more challenging way to thread beads onto twisted wire is to start at the stage where you separate your wires, then make a fold in one of the wires (D), slide a bead or beads onto the folded wire (E), twist the folded wire until the twist in the folded strand meets up with the original twisted and beaded strand, and finally, twist the two original wires together (F). Add beads and twist wire until you reach your next preferred length.

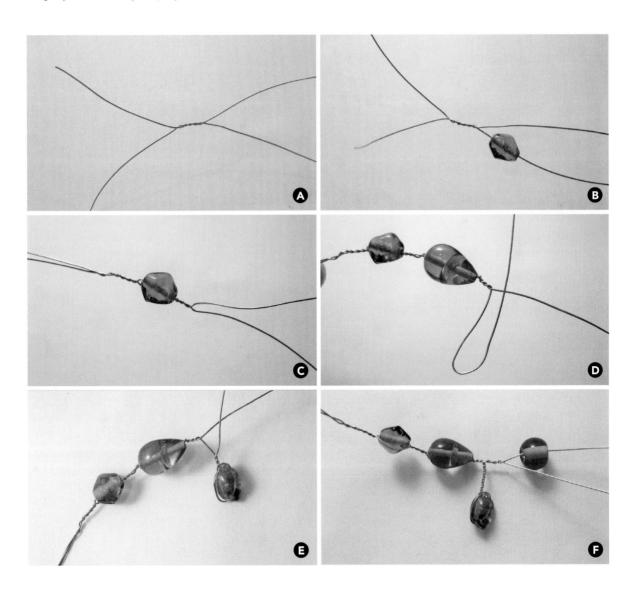

projects

Now that you know how to make your own beads, charms, and pendants and can identify and use the materials and tools in this book, you're ready to make the projects in this section. The projects are arranged in order of skill level from one to three. If you have mastered the basics of beading or have past experience with beadwork, then you are probably ready to tackle any project. If this is your first time working with beads and wire, start with a simpler project and work your way up.

skill level 1

Fusible Bead Projects

Fusible bead patterns can be found online by the hundreds, and the beads can be used to make coasters, magnets, window clings, and more. Perler is the most common brand of fusible beads sold in the U.S. The U.K. brand of fusible beads is Hama. Here are three additional ways to create with them.

You Will Need

Fusible beads for mustache:
- 100 dark brown beads
- 12 light brown beads

Fusible beads for peacock feather:
- 1 mint green bead
- 37 kelly green beads
- 52 hunter green beads
- 50 lime green beads
- 51 teal beads
- 13 blue beads
- 10 medium blue beads
- 11 dark blue beads
- 3 purple beads
- 23 orange beads
- 18 brown beads
- Fusible bead peg board
- ironing paper
- iron
- 1 large jump ring
- 1 plastic hook
- flat-nose pliers

Mustache and Peacock-Feather Backpack Clips

Directions

1 Follow the pattern of your choice (A, B) to place the fusible beads on the peg board (C). Follow the manufacturer's instructions for placing the ironing paper over the design and fusing the beads together (D). Always ask for adult help with the iron.

2 Open the jump ring by twisting it open with your fingers or flat-nose pliers, and thread it through the fusible bead hole as indicated on the pattern (or use a pin to reopen the hole if the iron melted it closed).

3 Hook the plastic hook loop onto the jump ring, and twist the jump ring closed.

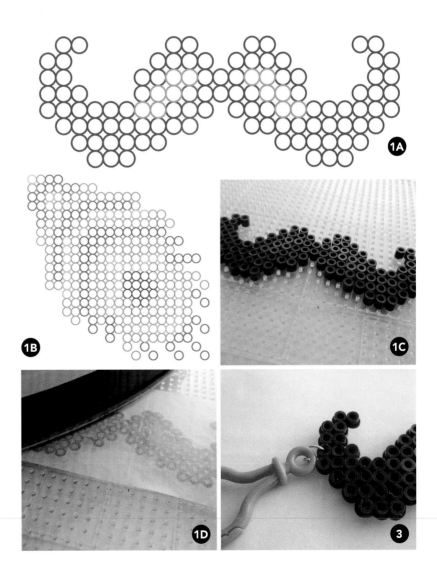

You Will Need

Fusible beads for 2 earrings:

- 24 yellow beads
- 12 orange beads
- 2 red beads
- fusible bead circle Peg-Board
- ironing paper
- iron
- 2 medium jump rings
- 2 small jump rings
- 2 ear wires

Marigold Earrings

Directions

1 Follow the pattern to place the fusible beads on the peg board for each earring. Follow the manufacturer's instructions for placing the ironing paper over the design and fusing the beads together. Always ask for adult help with the iron.

2 Twist open a medium jump ring with your fingers or flat-nose pliers, and thread it through the fusible bead hole (A) (or use a pin to reopen the hole if the iron melted it closed). Hook a small jump ring onto the medium jump ring, and use the flat-nose pliers to close the medium jump ring (B).

3 Use the flat-nose pliers to open the ear wire loop and hook it onto the small jump ring. Then, use the flat-nose pliers to close the loop on the ear wire. Repeat steps 2 and 3 for the other earring.

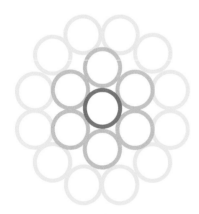

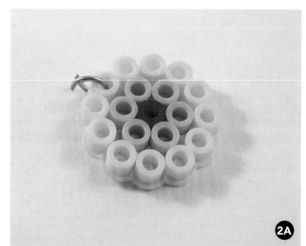

You Will Need

- ear buds
- approximately 140 fusible beads
- craft mat
- craft knife (requires adult assistance)

Ear Buds Cord Cover

Directions

1 Have an adult place a fusible bead flat side down on a craft mat or other cutting surface and slice through the length of the bead with a craft knife. Repeat for as many fusible beads as are needed to cover the ear bud wires (from the jack up to the point where the wire splits).

2 Pull apart the fusible bead slightly and push the wire through the cut opening of the fusible bead, starting near the jack on the ear buds. Work your way up with additional fusible beads, which will reform around the ear bud cord.

Fairy Bubble Wand

Blow bubbles in style. Forget cheap plastic bottles and wands. This simple project can be made quickly and with very few supplies. Make several and give them to friends with a jar of homemade colorful bubble solution.

You Will Need

- 14" (35.5 cm) of 18-gauge colored copper wire
- cylinder approximately 6" (15 cm) around
- various plastic beads (plan for 13 beads)
- wire cutters
- round-nose pliers
- 2 or 3 strips of 12" (30.5 cm) long narrow ribbon

Directions

1 Join the two ends of the 18-gauge wire so that you can find the center of the wire. Do not fold the wire but wrap the wire—starting at the center point of the wire—around a cylinder that is approximately 6" (15 cm) around. This can be something around the house such as a spice container or jelly jar. With the wire wrapped around the cylinder, twist the two ends of wire together three times firmly against the cylinder. Remove wire from cylinder.

2 Keeping the two pieces of wire together, thread several beads up to the twisted area of the wire until the handle is the preferred length (about 3 ½" [9 cm]), leaving approximately ½" (13 mm) of wire at the end. Use the wire cutters to trim off any excess.

3 Use the widest part of the round-nose pliers to create a loop at the end of the handle (A, B). You can even experiment with twisting the wire in some other way to create a fancy design. Just don't repeatedly bend the wire too much or it could weaken and break.

4 Fold the 12" (30.5)-long strips of ribbon in half, and push the folded part of the ribbon through the metal loop at the end of the bubble wand.

5 Put all the ribbon ends through the folded ribbon loop that is sticking out of the metal loop at the end of the bubble wand.

6 Gently pull on the ribbon ends to tighten the looped ribbons around the metal loop at the end of the bubble wand (A, B).

3A

3B

4

5

6A

6B

 skill level **1**

Seashell Wind Chimes

Save seashells and sea glass from trips to the ocean, so you can make a lasting memory of your vacation. Let the beads clink together in the wind or hang the wind chimes in a window so the light can pass through the glass beads.

You Will Need

- 1 large sturdy seashell

- several small seashells, sea glass, coral, and other beach finds

- glass beads of all shapes and colors (purchase a tub of mixed glass beads at your local craft store)

- several feet of natural jute twine

- rotary tool with 7/64" drill bit

- scissors

- pencil or toothpick

Directions

1 Have an adult use a rotary tool to drill 2 holes at the top of the seashell (for hanging the wind chimes) (A) and holes evenly spaced along the bottom edge of the seashell (B). Be sure to keep the shell surface wet in order to prevent overheating the tool and wearing out the drill bit.

2 Cut several 18" (0.5 m) pieces of jute twine per the number of holes that were drilled, and tie one end of each piece securely through the bottom holes in the seashell using a regular knot. Thread a bead onto the jute before securing the knot to help hide the holes.

3 One at a time, thread a glass bead onto the jute, spaced approximately 1" (2.5 cm) from the first knot, and tie another knot. Continue adding beads in this manner (A). To add shells or other beach findings, either drill a hole in the finding or wrap the jute around the item and tie it securely (B). This may require a bit of experimenting because beach findings can be so many different sizes and shapes. Add beads and beach findings until you reach the end of the piece of jute. Tie one last knot. Continue beading and tying beach findings to the other strands of jute, varying colors and objects as you go. *Note: Save heavier findings or beads for the ends of the string to straighten the strands when the wind chimes are hanging.*

4 Cut a 6" (15 cm) length of jute for hanging the wind chimes. Thread the jute through the two top holes, add a bead to each side, and knot the ends as you did with the other strands. Trim the excess pieces of jute. Add a dot of craft glue to the knots in the jute for reinforcement.

1A

1B

skill level
1

Candy Necklace Party Favor

Get a party started with a delectable swag of mixed candy pieces for the guests. If something less sweet is in order, then colorful cereal can be used in place of candy. Make a long-lasting necklace using other bright nonfood objects like pom-poms, glittered foam balls, and fabric strips.

You Will Need

- 15" (38 cm) of ¼" (6 mm)-wide ribbon (for threading candy)

- 18" (46 cm) of ¼" (6 mm)-wide ribbon (for around the neck)

- various candies and bright objects such as colored pasta, pom-poms, gummy creatures/shapes (gumdrops), glittered foam balls, fabric strips, circus peanuts, striped gum, and licorice

- plastic sewing needle

- scissors

Directions

1 Thread one end of the 15" (38 cm) piece of ribbon through the plastic sewing needle. Use the plastic sewing needle to create holes in soft candy and pieces that don't have holes.

2 Push the candy pieces down the piece of ribbon, leaving 3" (7.5 cm) of ribbon at the end without candy (A). (This may get a bit sticky, but do your best to keep your hands clean and dry.) Alternate pieces until approximately 3" (7.5 cm) of ribbon are left on the other end of the ribbon (B). Remove the plastic needle, and rinse off the end of the ribbon to remove any sticky goo from the candy.

3 Tie the ends of the 18" (46 cm) piece of ribbon to the ends of the 15" (38 cm) piece of ribbon. Use scissors to trim any excess ribbon, or leave the ribbon ends to accessorize the necklace.

skill level 1

Friendship Charm Pin

Look for charms and colored beads that match your friends' personalities—initials, hobbies, birthstones, favorite colors, school activities—and make detachable charms that can be given away or traded for a collection that can be worn proudly on a jacket, a bag, or shoelaces.

You Will Need

- 1 charm pin or large safety pin
- small decorative beads
- metal charms
- eye pins (one for each hanging charm)
- lobster clasps (one for each hanging charm)
- head pins (one for each beaded strand charm)
- hollow spacer (for holding extra hanging charms)
- wire cutters
- flat-nose pliers
- round-nose pliers

Directions

The following directions are for three different types of hanging charms for a friendship pin, but use your imagination to come up with still dozens more ideas for accessorizing a friendship pin with detachable charms.

1 Choose a charm and add it to the eye of an eye pin by using flat-nose pliers to open and close the eye with the charm in place (refer to the instructions for a jump ring on page 45).

2 Add beads to the eye pin, but leave approximately ¼" (6 mm) of the wire unbeaded. Use wire cutters to trim any excess wire.

3 Use the round-nose pliers to create a loop with the excess wire of the eye pin. Before closing the loop, thread a lobster clasp onto the wire, making sure the opening of the clasp faces the back of the charm (A). Use the flat-nose pliers to close the loop (B). This completes one charm.

4 To make a beaded strand charm, start with step 2 but add the beads to a head pin, not an eye pin (A). Then, leave ¼" (6 mm) of the pin unbeaded to make the loop (B) and attach the lobster clasp.

(continued)

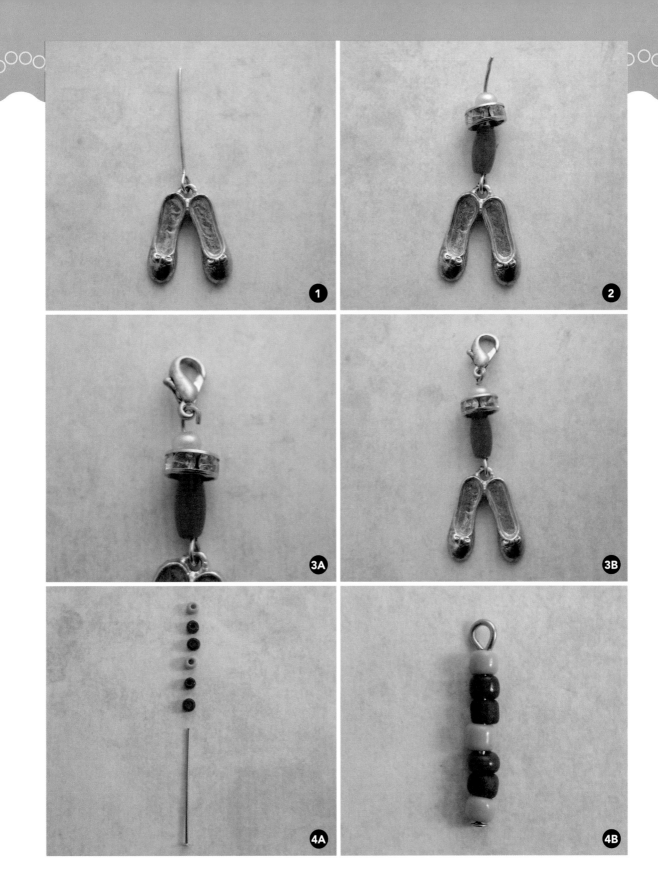

5 To make a charm using a hollow spacer for hanging extra charms, use two head pins. Thread the head pins through each end of the spacer from the inside out. The head pin designated for the top of the charm will get trimmed to ¼" (6 mm) and then looped to attach the lobster clasp. The head pin designated for the bottom of the charm will get trimmed to ¼" (6 mm) and then looped to attach a charm (A). If the head pins are too small for the spacer holes and pull through the holes, thread a seed bead onto each head pin before threading it through the spacer holes, and that will keep the head pins in place (B).

5A

5B

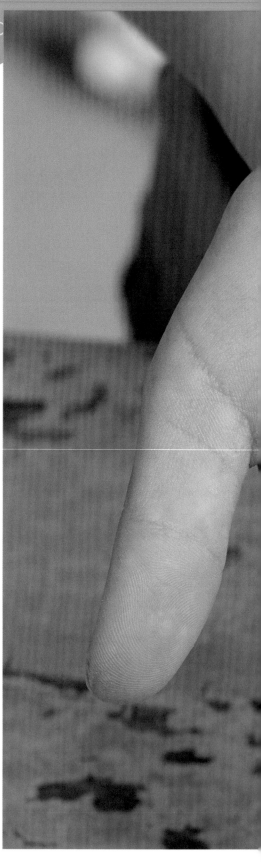

Seasonal Zipper Pulls

Add some dazzle to a jacket, cosmetic bag, or anything else that has a zipper. The snowman zipper pull matches everything, and the dragonfly zipper pull lets your imagination soar with color options.

Snowman

You Will Need

- 1 small metal hook

- 1 head pin

- one 7-mm jump ring

- one 7-mm glass snowman head bead (see Resources, page 126)

- two 10-mm round white glass beads

- one 5 × 10-mm black rondelle (disc-shaped) bead

- one 6-mm black cube bead

- 2" (5 cm) of fuzzy yarn

- round-nose pliers

- wire cutters

- *Note:* Other snowman beads are available online; some have earmuffs and therefore could be used in place of the plain snowman head bead, the black cube bead, and the disc-shaped bead.

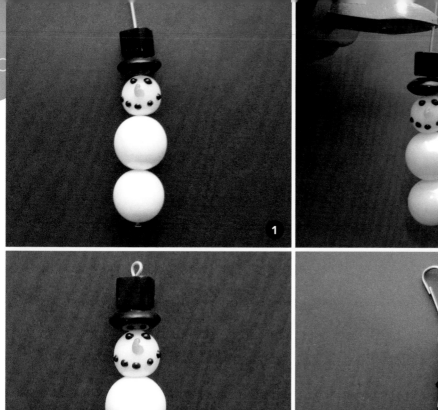

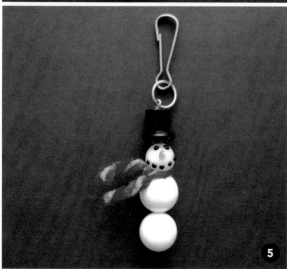

Directions

1 Thread the following beads onto the head pin in this order: two 10-mm round white glass beads, one 7-mm glass snowman head bead, one 5 × 10-mm black rondelle bead, one 6-mm black cube bead.

2 Use the wire cutters to cut the excess wire so that approximately ¼" (6 mm) of wire remains.

3 Use the round-nose pliers to create a loop at the top of the snowman's hat.

4 Twist open the jump ring (see page 45 for directions on opening and closing a jump ring), and thread it through the wire loop at the top of the snowman's hat as well as the loop at the base of the metal hook. Close the jump ring.

5 Tie the 2" (5 cm) strand of yarn around the snowman's neck and pull the two strands to the side, trimming the excess yarn so that the "scarf" is proportional to the snowman.

Dragonfly

You Will Need

- 1 small metal hook
- 1 head pin
- one 7-mm jump ring
- 12" (30.5 cm) of 26-gauge wire
- various seed beads for wings
- various colorful beads approximately 5 mm wide (round, rondelle, tube, or E beads) for the body
- round-nose pliers
- wire cutters

Directions

1 Thread the various 5-mm beads onto the head pin so that the body of the dragonfly is 2" (5 cm) long.

2 Use the wire cutters to cut the excess wire so that approximately ¼" (6 mm) of wire remains.

(continued)

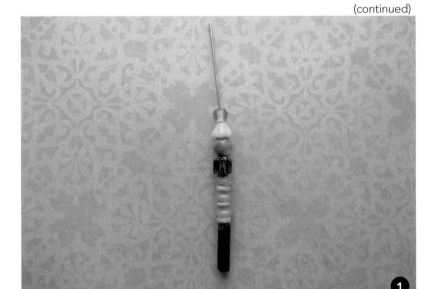

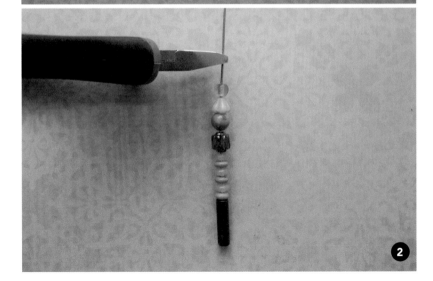

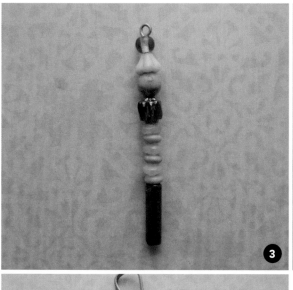

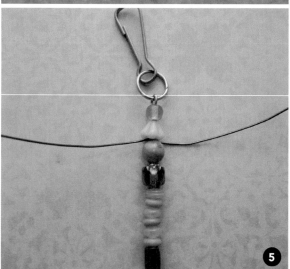

3 Use the round-nose pliers to create a loop at the top/head of the dragonfly.

4 Twist open the jump ring (see page 45 for instructions) and thread it through the wire loop at the top of the dragonfly's head as well as the loop at the base of the metal hook. Close the jump ring.

5 Center the 12" (30.5 cm) piece of 26-gauge wire between two beads approximately ¼" to ⅓" (6 to 9 mm) down from the dragonfly's head. Then, wrap the wires behind the dragonfly, crisscrossing them in the back, and bring them to the front of the dragonfly. Pull tightly.

6 Starting with one strand of wire, thread seed beads onto the wire (A), folding the wire back in toward the dragonfly's body once half of the wire has been beaded (B). By folding the wire in toward the body, you have created a dragonfly wing.

7 Loop the wire from the front around to the back and then to the front again, being sure to loop the wire between the same two beads where the wire was originally centered (A, B). Keep everything tight so that the beads don't shift around. This will also en-sure that the wires that are wrapped around the body of the dragonfly don't get loose and come undone.

(continued)

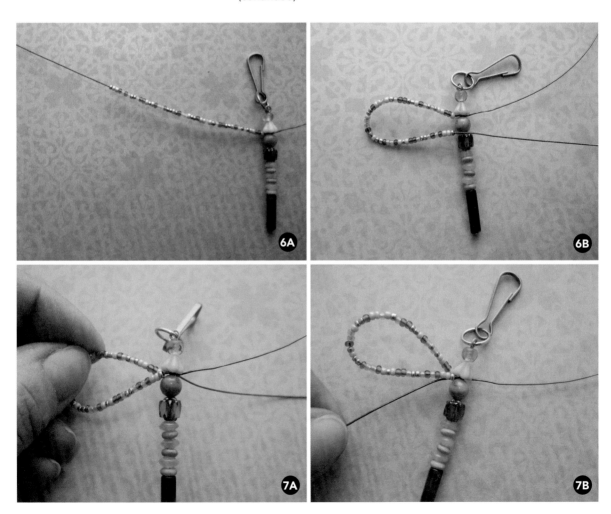

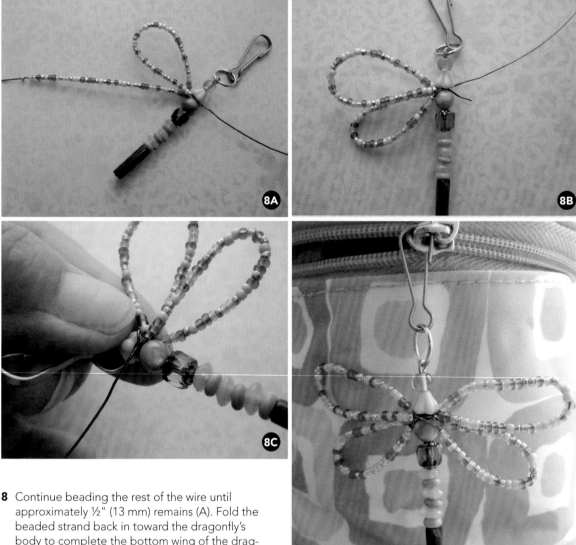

8 Continue beading the rest of the wire until approximately ½" (13 mm) remains (A). Fold the beaded strand back in toward the dragonfly's body to complete the bottom wing of the dragonfly (B). Wrap the wire as before (to the back and then toward the front), but hide the excess wire by tucking it between the wings and the body of the dragonfly. If wire is still visible, use the wire cutters to trim it off (C).

9 Continue from step 6 with the other side of the dragonfly. If the ends of the wires are being stubborn, use a pair of flat-nose pliers to grip and pull or wrap them to get them to snugly fit where they need to go. Place a dot of craft or jewelry glue at the source of the wire wrapping to keep particularly messy wires in place. Wire wrapping takes practice, and if you are just starting out, be patient when working the wire in and around other pieces. Eventually, you'll become a pro!

You Will Need

- four 6" (15 cm) pieces of colorful coated wire
- 1 large bead with at least 3-mm-diameter hole
- 4 eyeball beads
- 2 bump pipe cleaner segments
- four 4-mm round beads or E beads
- craft glue
- skinny dowel (or pencil) for making twirled antennae

Cootie Bug Study Buddy

skill level **2**

Make this alien friend to accessorize your desktop while you do homework, or give one to a friend. Make a whole army of cootie bugs to guard your windowsill! Cooties are fun and easy to make, and the more of them you make, the easier they will be to put together.

Directions

1 Place the four pieces of 6" (15 cm) wire side by side and then twist the wires together, leaving about 2 ½" (6 cm) of wires at one end. Make sure the twist is tight enough so that the wires stay together when you are done twisting. The twisted part of the wires will be hidden inside the large body bead. The shorter pieces of wire at one end will be the legs of your cootie bug, and the longer pieces of wire will be used for the antennae and eyes.

2 Slide the large bead onto all four wires and position it over the twist in the wires. Then, spread out the shorter wires of your cootie in four different directions. These are the legs.

3 Slide one 4-mm round bead onto each of the four legs and keep it close to the end. Use your fingers to fold the end of the wire up until it touches the rest of the leg wire so that the round bead is secured at the end of the wire as a cootie foot.

4 Now, adjust the legs for standing position by creating a knee bend and then bending each of the feet slightly. Picture the legs of a fancy chair.

5 Slide one eyeball bead not quite halfway down one of the long wires (A). Then, fold the wire down (B). Twist the folded wire like a twist tie by holding the eyeball bead at one end and the two wires together at the other end (C). This secures the eye bead. Repeat with a second eyeball bead.

(continued)

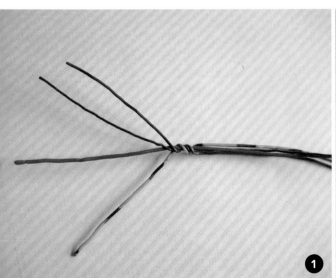

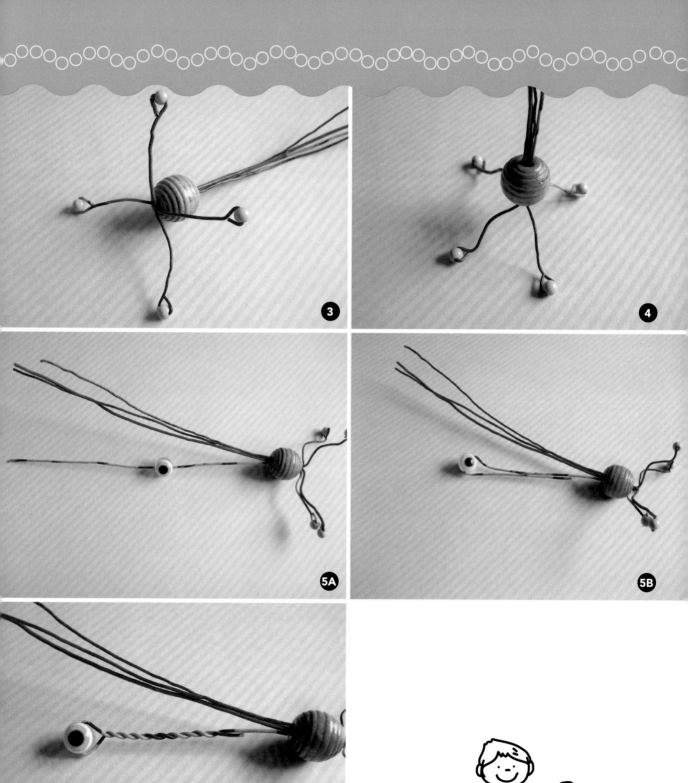

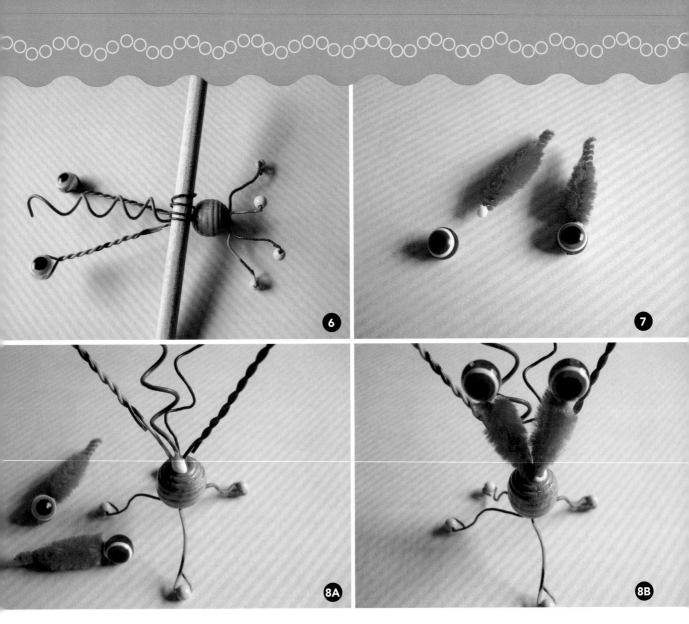

6 Starting at one end of each of the two remaining wires, wrap the wire around the skinny dowel all the way to the body bead. Remove the dowel and adjust the antenna so that it looks like a long spring. Repeat with the other remaining wire.

7 Apply a dot of glue to the tip of each bump pipe cleaner and slide the remaining two eyeball beads onto the tips so that the pipe cleaners remain on the inside of the eyeball beads. Allow to dry.

8 Apply a dot of glue to the top opening of the body bead and fit the two narrowest ends of the bump pipe cleaners into the hole (A, B). Allow to dry.

9 When the glue has dried, adjust the eyes, antennae, and legs.

Tip For other cootie bugs, consider making the eye wires shorter and using longer, fluffier bump pipe cleaners for the background eyes. Either way, one set of eyes will be shorter than the other set of eyes, giving your cootie bug a funny alien look.

School Spirit Utility Fob

Working with parachute cord is as easy as 1, 2, 3. This simple utility fob can be made with cording in school colors (rather than yellow and black). Then, hang useful gadgets like a flashlight, small tools, a tube of lip balm, and more. The hook is ideal for attaching to a belt loop or bag.

You Will Need

- 4' (1.2 m) of yellow 550 parachute cord
- 4' (1.2 m) of black 550 parachute cord
- 6 spacer hoops with a ½" (13 mm) hole
- 1 small key ring
- 1 swivel hook with ⅞" (22 mm) ring
- scissors
- lighter or match

Directions

1 Fold each 4' (1.2 m) piece of colored parachute cord in half and make a loop through the swivel hook ring. Place the two different colors of looped cord next to each other. Once they are looped, four strands will be hanging from the swivel hook.

2 Turn so the hook hangs down. Fold the two gold cords into a loop, and wrap the two black cords around the base of the loop.

(continued)

3 Make a loop with the two black cords and insert the loop into the gold loop (A). Then, pull the gold loop tightly to secure the black loop (B).

4 Thread a spacer hoop onto both strands of gold cord. Then, fold the gold cord into a loop and insert it into the black loop (A). Pull the black loop tightly to secure the gold loop (B).

5 Thread a spacer hoop onto both strands of black cord. Then, as before, fold the black cord into a loop and insert it into the gold loop (A). Pull the gold loop tightly to secure the black loop (B). Make the next two knots of black and gold without adding spacers. Then, add spacers to the next two knots that follow. Continue adding knots until 6 spacers have been added and one more knot of each color follows without a spacer.

(continued)

3A

3B

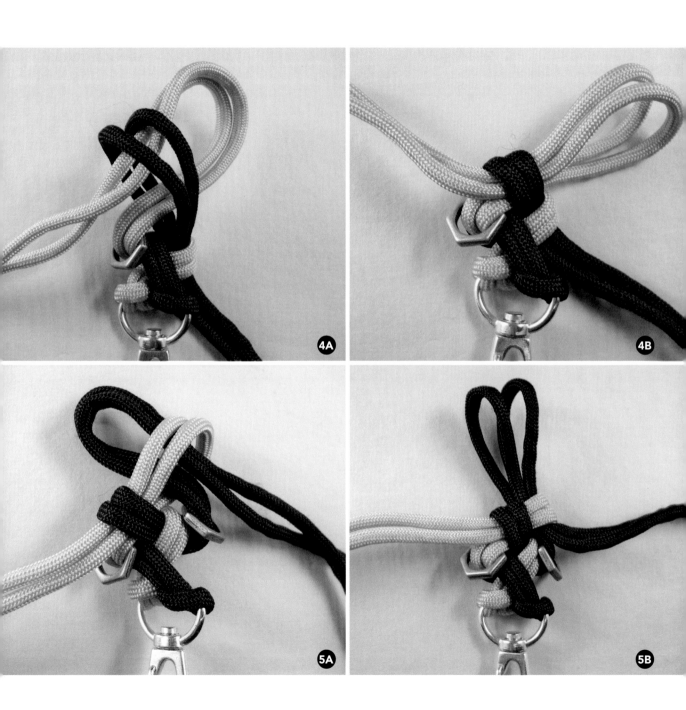

6 To finish the ends of the parachute cord, add a small key ring to both strands of gold parachute cord before inserting the looped cord into the black loop (A). Pull the black loop to secure the gold loop, leaving a bit of space in the gold loop for the next step (B).

7 Insert the ends of the black cord through the gold loop from the right side, and insert the ends of the gold cord through the gold loop from the left side (A). Pull the gold loop tightly to secure the ends in the gold loop (B).

8 Loop each remaining set of colored cord from the outside of the key ring, around the back, and in through the center of the key ring (A). Pull the ends snugly (B).

9 Use the scissors to trim back the ends of the parachute cord (A). Have an adult use a lighter or match to singe the ends of the parachute cord so that they melt together (B).

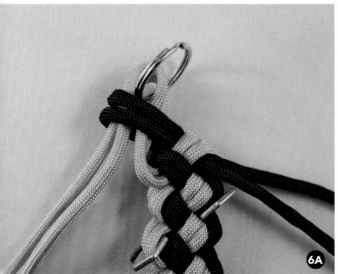

6A

6B

You Will Need

- 4 to 5 coils of bracelet memory wire

- assorted beads and spacers

- 2 medium jump rings

- 1 small jump ring

- 1 watch face with top and bottom loops (pendant holes) (see Resources, page 126)

- 1 hook clasp

- round-nose pliers

- wire cutters

- *Optional:* one or two 6" (15 cm) pieces of thin organza ribbon

skill level
2

Twirly Whirly Watch Bracelet

The Twirly Whirly Watch Bracelet can be created in styles ranging from fun to sophisticated. Use colorful acrylic beads for a youthful look and glass or metal beads for a fashionable flair.

Directions

1 Attach the medium jump rings to the top and bottom loops of the watch face, following instructions for opening and closing jump rings on page 45.

2 Attach the small jump ring to the medium jump ring through the top loop of the watch face. Attach the hook clasp to the small jump ring.

(continued)

3 Use the round-nose pliers to create a loop at one end of the memory wire. Attach the looped memory wire to the jump ring that runs through the bottom loop of the watch face so that the outside coil of the wire is facing out along with the watch face.

4 Begin beading the memory wire. Alternate styles and sizes of beads until the bracelet coils twice around the wrist. Keep in mind that the hook at the top of the watch face is the closure that attaches to the opposite end of the memory wire once it has been beaded and coiled around the wrist, so stop beading the memory wire when the top of the watch meets up with the end of the beaded memory wire. **Note:** Wrap the wire around your wrist to judge how long to bead the memory wire.)

5 When the coils are the preferred length, use the wire cutters to cut the excess memory wire so that ½" (13 mm) remains.

6 Use the round-nose pliers to create a sideways loop. To put on the bracelet, attach the hook clasp in the top of the watch to the sideways loop of the memory wire. The bracelet should be slightly loose like a bangle.

7 *Optional:* Tie one or two pieces of 6" (15 cm) organza ribbon through the jump rings above and below the watch face to fill in the gaps where there are no beads.

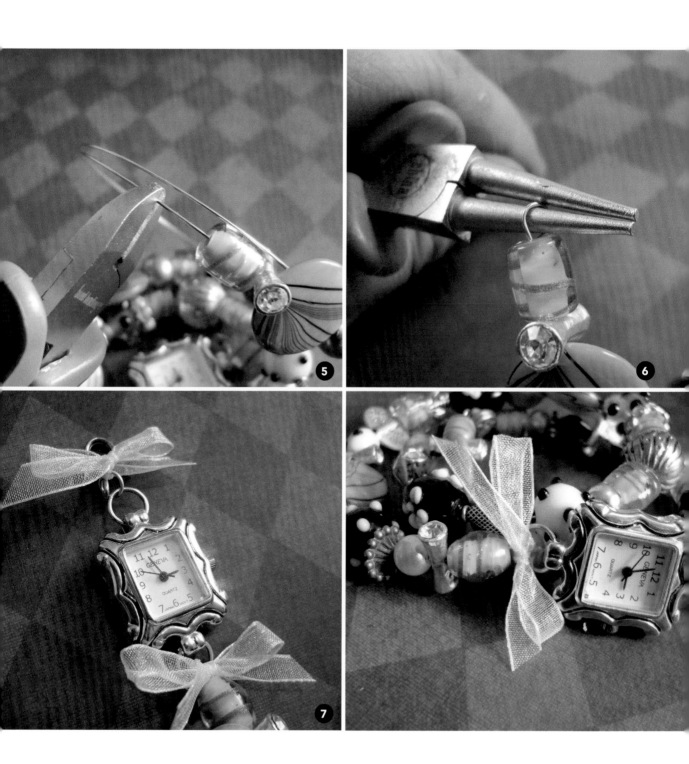

skill level 2

Button Ring

Make this quick piece of finger bling with colorful coated wire and assorted multicolored buttons stacked like a flower and accented with tiny bead baubles.

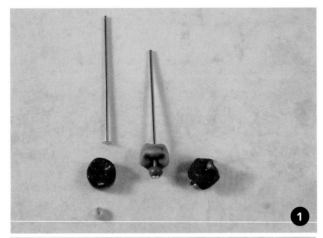

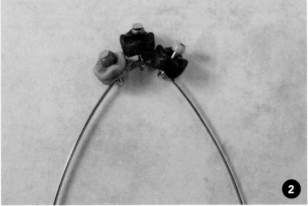

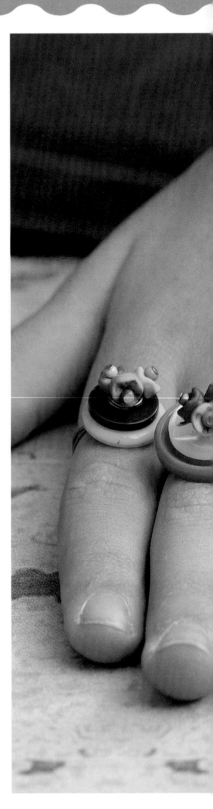

Directions

1 Make three tiny bead charms for the top of the button ring by threading one seed bead and one flower bead onto a head pin, using wire cutters to trim the excess wire back to ¼" (6 mm) and using round-nose pliers to create a small closed loop at the end of the head pin. (See page 45 for creating a loop with round-nose pliers.)

2 Find the halfway point of the 6" (15 cm) piece of wire and thread the beaded head pins to the halfway point.

(continued)

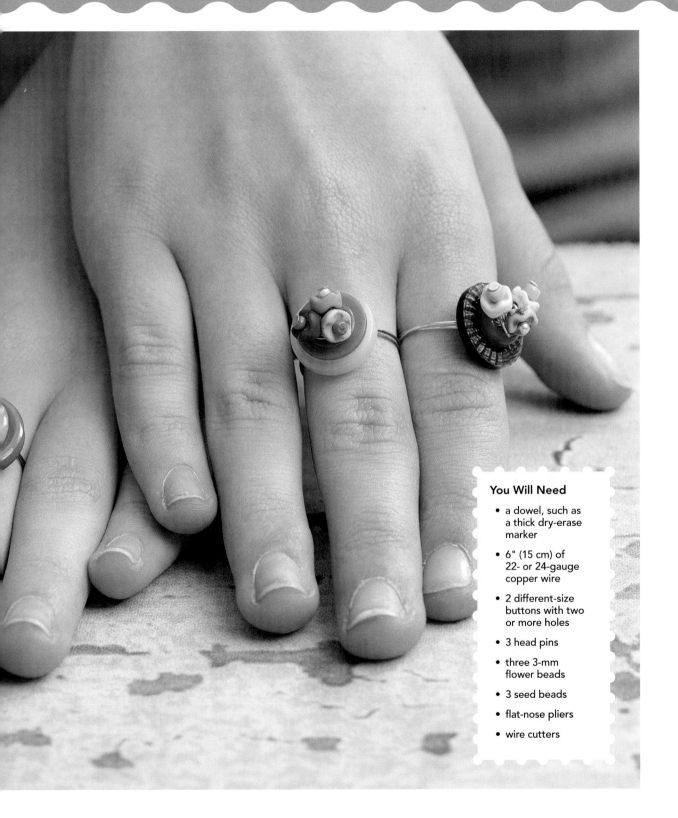

You Will Need

- a dowel, such as a thick dry-erase marker
- 6" (15 cm) of 22- or 24-gauge copper wire
- 2 different-size buttons with two or more holes
- 3 head pins
- three 3-mm flower beads
- 3 seed beads
- flat-nose pliers
- wire cutters

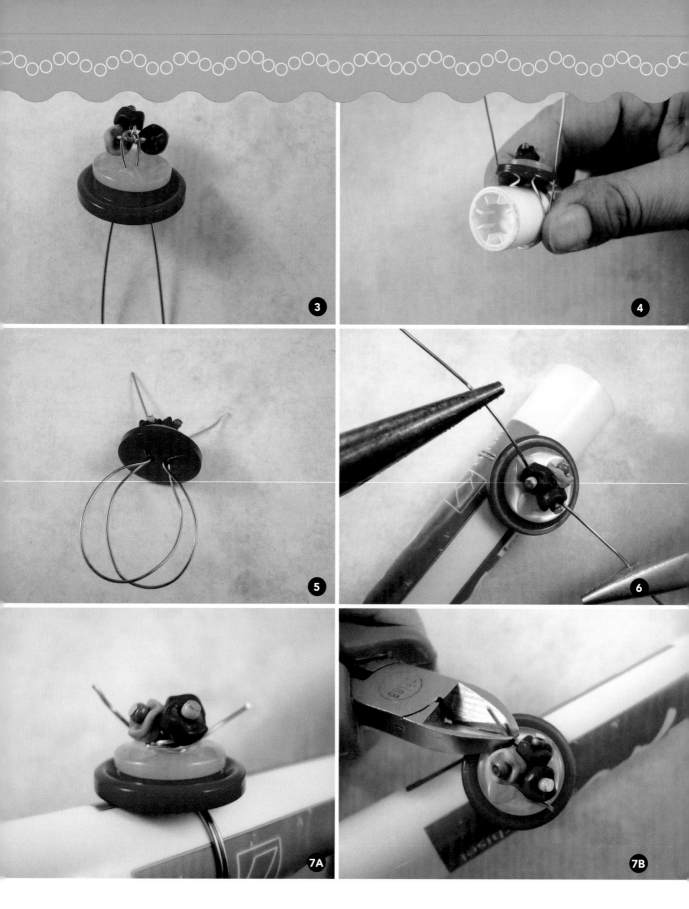

3 Stack two different-color, different-size buttons together. Then, run each end of wire down through each of the two holes in the buttons, keeping the beaded head pins on the central part of the wire.

4 Use a thick marker or a dowel that is about the thickness of a finger for wrapping the wire. Hold the buttons against the marker and bring each wire from one side around to the other side, then straight up.

5 Remove the ring from the marker to insert the two wire ends up through the button holes they are facing.

6 Return the ring to the marker. Then, use two pairs of flat-nose pliers (even round-nose pliers will work) to pull the two wires tightly up through the buttonholes and out to the sides. This will tighten the wires and make them more uniformly round.

7 Wrap each wire end tightly around the base of the cluster of beaded head pins (A), and use wire cutters to trim off the excess wire (B).

skill level
3

Pop Star Tiara

The pipe cleaner tiara is fit for a pop star or a princess. Follow these instructions for using fluorescent pipe cleaners and star beads, or change up the project with glittery metallic pipe cleaners and metallic beads.

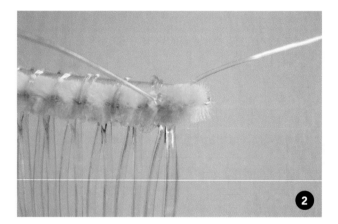

Directions

1 If necessary, cut a large hair comb in half to make two smaller hair combs for this project.

2 The regular green pipe cleaner is the bottom piece of the tiara that will be placed on a head. Lay one hair comb against the end of the regular green pipe cleaner, making sure the hair comb is placed on what will be the inside of the tiara. Tie one end of one piece of jelly cord between the first two tines of the hair comb and the pipe cleaner to hold the hair comb in place. Make two knots. Wind the jelly cord in between the hair comb tines and around the pipe cleaner, working from one end to the other and then back again until the two ends of jelly cord meet. Tie the two ends of jelly cord together several times into a secure knot. Repeat with the other comb on the other end of the pipe cleaner.

(continued)

You Will Need

- 2 small hair combs or 1 large hair comb cut in half

- 1 regular green pipe cleaner

- 2 skinny green pipe cleaners

- 1 skinny orange pipe cleaner

- 1 skinny pink pipe cleaner

- 1 skinny purple pipe cleaner

- 1 large acrylic stacking flower bead

- 2 round acrylic faceted beads

- 3 acrylic star beads

- 7 acrylic teardrop beads

- two 12" (30.5 cm) pieces of clear jelly cord or stretchy cord

- scissors

3 Measure 3" (7.5 cm) from the end of the regular green pipe cleaner and twist the end of a skinny green pipe cleaner with the regular green pipe cleaner.

4 Slide on a star bead before making a 2" (5 cm)-high loop with the skinny green pipe cleaner. Then, thread the skinny green pipe cleaner back down through the star bead. Wrap the skinny green pipe cleaner around the regular green pipe cleaner and bring the excess skinny green pipe cleaner back up at an angle. (The end of this pipe cleaner will be finished in a later step.) Repeat steps 3 and 4 on the opposite end of the regular green pipe cleaner with the other skinny green pipe cleaner.

5 Wrap the skinny pink pipe cleaner around the regular green pipe cleaner where the hair comb ends, Then, guide the skinny pink pipe cleaner *up* through the star bead on the 2" (5 cm)-high green loop.

6 Guide the skinny pink pipe cleaner *down* through the star bead on the 2" (5 cm)-high green loop on the *opposite* side of the tiara, and twist the end with the regular green pipe cleaner where the hair comb ends.

7 Slide the large acrylic flower bead onto both pieces of skinny green pipe cleaner halfway between the base of the tiara and the arc in the skinny pink pipe cleaner.

8 Wrap each piece of excess skinny green pipe cleaner once around the skinny pink pipe cleaner at an angle. Slide a round, faceted bead onto each excess skinny green pipe cleaner. Finally, curve each end of the pipe cleaner into a loop with your fingers.

(continued)

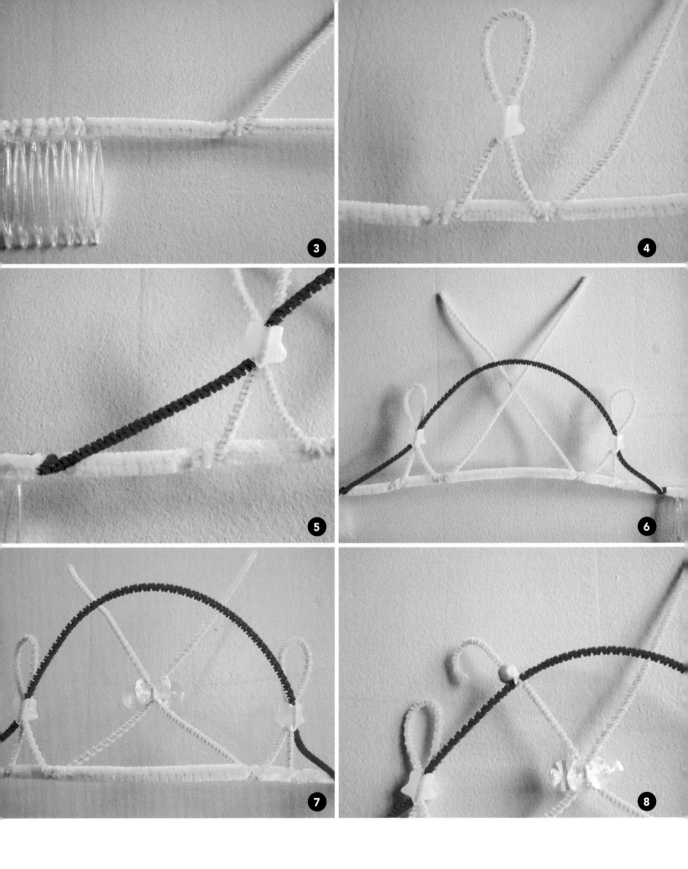

9 Wrap the end of the skinny purple pipe cleaner around the regular green pipe cleaner between the 2" (5 cm)-high green loop and where the excess skinny green pipe cleaner moves up at an angle. Slide on three acrylic teardrop beads and space them evenly.

10 Now, wrap the skinny purple pipe cleaner around the centermost point of the skinny pink pipe cleaner at the top of the tiara (A). Slide an acrylic star bead onto the skinny purple pipe cleaner. Then, bend the skinny purple pipe cleaner and guide the end back down through the acrylic star bead to form a 1 ½" (4 cm)-high loop (B). Slide on three more acrylic teardrop beads and space them evenly. Then, wrap the end of the skinny purple pipe cleaner around the regular green pipe cleaner in the space between the 2" (5 cm)-high green loop and where the excess skinny green pipe cleaner moves up at an angle *on the opposite side of the tiara*. Cut off any extra pipe cleaner with a pair of scissors.

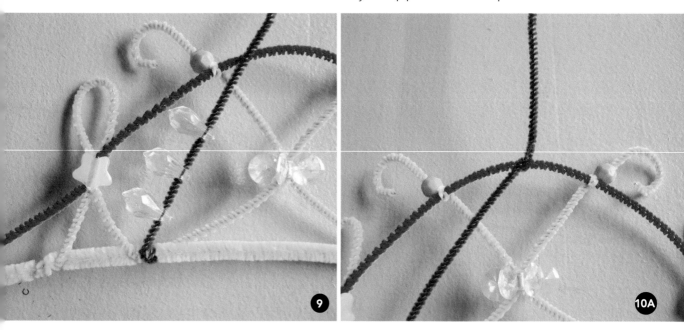

11 Thread one acrylic teardrop bead onto the halfway point of the skinny orange pipe cleaner. Center the skinny orange pipe cleaner in the space under the acrylic flower bead and between the skinny green pipe cleaners. Then, wrap each end of the skinny orange pipe cleaner around the regular green pipe cleaner where the skinny green pipe cleaner is already wrapped. Wrap from front to back, back to front, and up to the back of the tiara.

12 Finally, guide the skinny orange pipe cleaner between the skinny green pipe cleaner loop and the skinny pink pipe cleaner arc and wrap it around the regular green pipe cleaner to secure it in place. Use the scissors to cut off any extra pipe cleaner. Curve the tiara to fit your head.

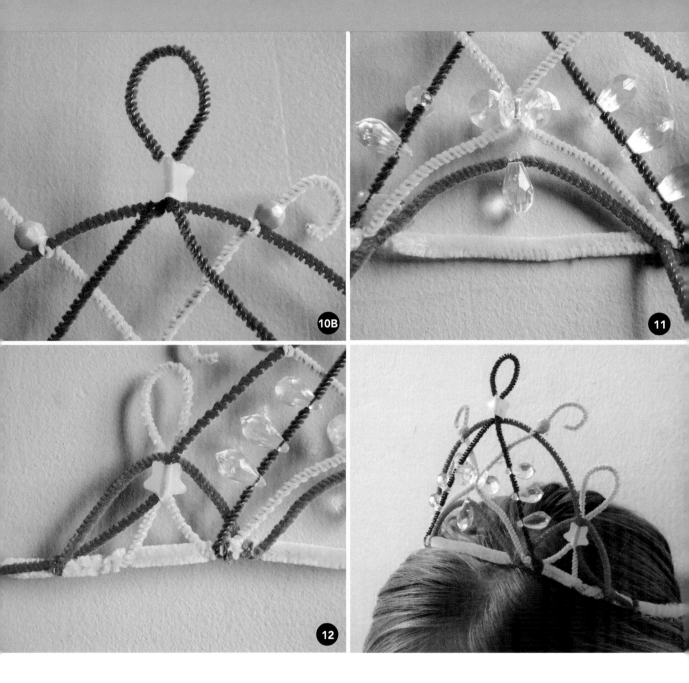

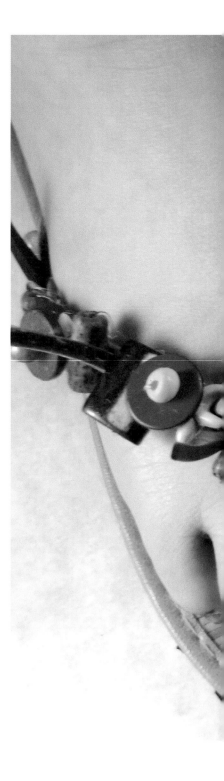

skill level 3

Beach Comber Flip-Flops

Colorful beads made from wood and coconut shells transform a pair of normal beach flip-flops into a summertime sensation. Inexpensive flip-flops can be purchased at a craft store and dressed up with shiny glass beads to be worn for a pedicure, too.

Directions

1 Tie one end of the jelly cord to the end of one strap of a flip-flop. Make at least three knots. Move the tied end of the jelly cord to the inside of the flip-flop. Bring the long piece of jelly cord from the inside of the flip-flop strap underneath the strap and up over the top of the strap.

2 Thread a round bead and disk bead onto the jelly cord (A). Then, thread the jelly cord twice through the first loop that you tied (B).

(continued)

3 Bring the long piece of jelly cord back under the inside of the strap to the outside of the strap, holding onto a loop of jelly cord on the inside of the strap. Thread a round bead and a pendant bead onto the jelly cord (or two other beads of your choice that are about the width of the flip-flop strap) (A). Then, thread the jelly cord twice through the loop of jelly cord from the last beaded section (B).

4 Continue adding beads to the jelly cord and looping the jelly cord around the flip-flop strap as in step 3. Alternate styles and colors of beads for a clustered, blended look. The back inside of the strap will have a consistent woven look from looping and beading the jelly cord.

5 When you reach the center of the flip-flop, be sure to continue looping the jelly cord to the inside of the flip-flop.

6 When you reach the end of both straps, tie off the jelly cord by looping and tying it several times through the last loop. Add a dot of craft glue to the knots at the beginning and end of each flip-flop to keep the knots from coming undone.

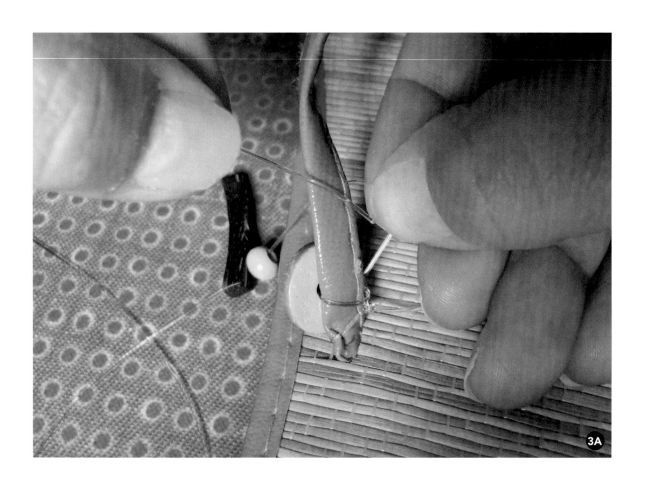

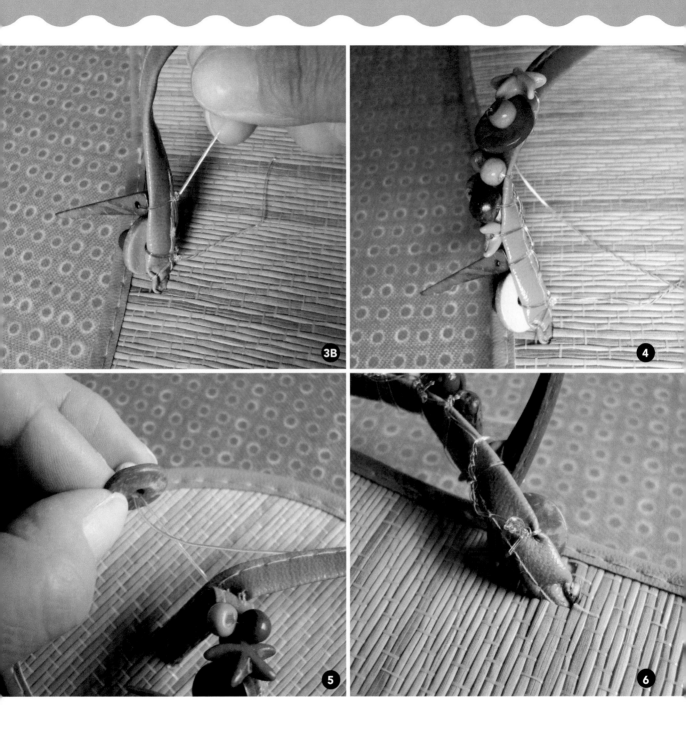

Crystal Night-Light Shade

This sophisticated night-light shade is a simple way to dress up a girl's bedroom. Crystal beads will cast soothing rainbows on the wall and drive away nighttime fears.

You Will Need

- 1 round night-light shade kit (see Resources, page 126)
- approximately twenty 6" (15 cm) pieces of 24-gauge silver-colored wire
- approximately twenty 4" (10 cm) strands of clear and crystal beads in varying widths and styles
- 9 crystal drop beads
- 21" (53 cm) of white feather trim
- wire cutters
- hot-glue gun

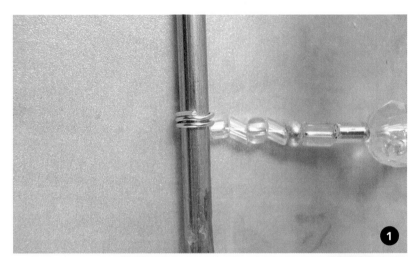

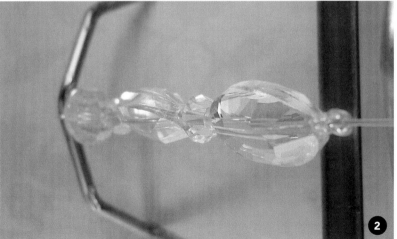

Directions

1 Work from the center of the night-light shade. Use your fingers to wrap one piece of 6" wire around the top metal rod of the shade and twist into place.

2 Thread a variety of beads onto the wire until they reach the bottom metal rod of the shade. Wrap and twist the remaining wire into place the same way as before. Use wire cutters to remove any excess wire.

(continued)

3 Follow steps 1 and 2 to bead more wires on either side of the center wire. Work from the center to the outside edge to be sure you balance the beads. When you are finished, look for spaces between strands of beads that are wide enough for another strand, and add strands as necessary. Use smaller beads to fill in open spaces so that the strands don't crowd each other.

4 When the shade is filled in with strands of beads, secure the crystal drop beads, evenly spaced, to the bottom rod of the shade with jump rings (A, B). See page 45 if you need to review how to open and close jump rings.

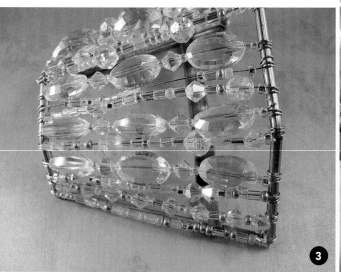

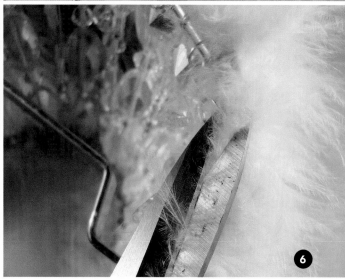

5 Have an adult hot glue the white feather trim to the shade, working across the top rod of the shade, down the side, across the bottom rod of the shade, and up the opposite side. This will hide all of the twisted wire ends and keep the crystal drop beads from sliding back and forth.

6 Use scissors along the bottom inside edge of the night-light shade to trim back the feathers so that the crystal drop beads are visible when hanging.

Macramé Skater Cuff

skill level 3

Black and olive jute twine are woven together with hitch knots to create this unique cuff perfect for both boys and girls. A twist-open belt closure and hex nuts add to the chunky appearance.

Directions

1 Fold each strand of jute in half and loop through one piece of the fashion buckle in order of black, green, black.

2 Tightly wrap a piece of clear tape around the ends of the green jute to keep them from fraying while you work.

(continued)

You Will Need

- Two 8' (2.5 m) pieces of 2-mm, 3-ply black jute

- 8' (2.5 m) of 2-mm, 3-ply green jute

- 15 hex nuts

- 1 fashion buckle with twist closure (See resources on page 126)

- clear tape

- scissors

3 Thread a hex nut onto the two pieces of green jute. Then, beginning with the green strands of jute in the center, loop them twice around the black strands of jute and pull them just tightly enough that there are no spaces between the loops (A, B). Use the illustration as a guide (C). It indicates the pattern for threading hex nuts and making knots, beginning with adding the hex nut, tying the green jute, tying the black jute, and continuing from there. Loops will always be made on strands 2 and 5.

4 Loop the two outside black strands of jute twice around strands 2 and 5 (also black) as shown in the illustration, and pull them firmly in place (A, B).

(continued)

3A

3B

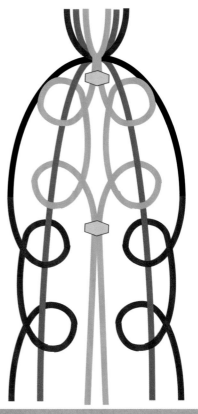

3C

4A

4B

5 Repeat the pattern of adding a hex nut, looping the green strands, and then looping the black strands according to the succession in the illustration until the cuff is the desired length for wearing on a wrist (about 15 hex nuts will be used). For the last row of the cuff, add a hex nut to the two center strands of green jute one last time and loop the outside black strands of jute once around strands 2 and 5 (also black).

6 Loop each set of strands through the other piece of the fashion buckle from underneath (A). Then, loop each set of strands down and between themselves so that the loose strands are now dangling at the back/inside of the cuff (B).

7 Tie strands 1 and 2 with strand 3. Tie strand 4 with strands 5 and 6. Make two knots. Tie strands 3 and 4 together twice. Use scissors to trim the excess jute from the back of the cuff.

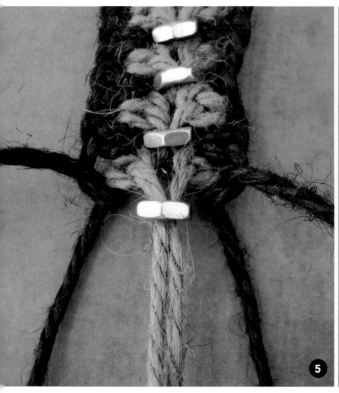

5

6A

6B

7

skill level

3

Daisy Chain Bookmark

This delicate and charming bookmark is connected to a loop of elastic so you can keep your place and not have to worry about your bookmark falling out. You can even add a clasp and jump ring to each end of the bookmark and wear it as a bracelet.

You Will Need

- 24" (61 cm) of 15-mm beading thread

- 2 small split rings

- 80 yellow seed beads (for 10 flowers)

- 10 large purple seed beads (for 10 flowers)

- 20 green seed beads (for 10 flowers and the long stem)

- 20 green drop beads (for 10 flowers)

- 10 green bugle beads (for the long stem)

- 12" (30.5 cm) of round elastic cord

- scissors

- *Optional:* 2 beads that will fit over two pieces of elastic (see step 8)

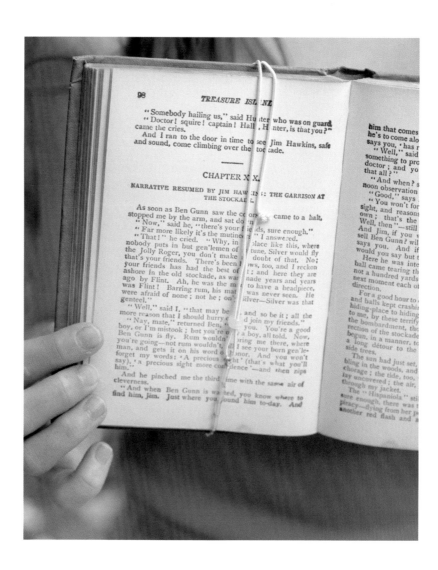

Directions

1 Tie the 24" (61 cm) piece of weaving thread onto one split ring. Make the knot as close to the split ring as you can. Use a scissors to cut the excess thread.

2 Slide eight yellow seed beads onto the weaving thread, and put the weaving thread through the first yellow seed bead (A). Refer to the illustration for the direction of the thread through all beads needed to make one complete flower (B).

3 Slide one purple seed bead onto the weaving thread, and put the weaving thread through the fourth yellow seed bead (A). Pull the beads into place (B).

4 Slide one green seed bead and one green drop bead onto the weaving thread, and put the weaving thread down through the third yellow seed bead on one side and then the green seed bead.

5 Slide one green drop bead onto the weaving thread, and put the weaving thread down through the third yellow seed bead on the other side of the flower and then the green seed bead. This completes one flower. Make a total of ten flowers.

(continued)

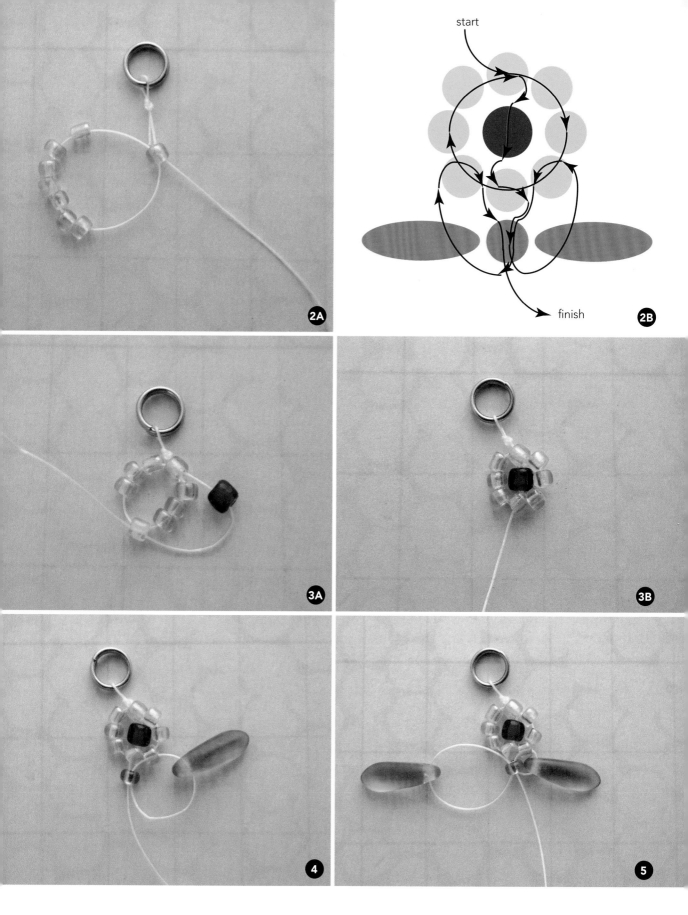

start

finish

2A

2B

3A

3B

4

5

6 Once you have made ten flowers, add alternating ten green bugle beads and ten green seed beads to make a long stem.

7 To finish off the beaded strand, loop it through the other split ring and make a knot, as you did in step 1, but double the knot this time. Use scissors to cut the excess thread.

8 Loop the 12" (30.5 cm) piece of elastic cord through both split rings. *Optional:* To add beads to the elastic, slide the beads onto the elastic before looping the cord through the split rings. Then, slide the elastic ends back through each bead (A). Knot the elastic tightly, and use scissors to trim the elastic close to the knot (B).

If working with seed beads is difficult because of their size, try working with pony beads and cotton cording to get the hang of how to loop the thread through the beads. In fact, if you have enough cotton cording to work with, you could make a daisy chain–pony bead belt!

6

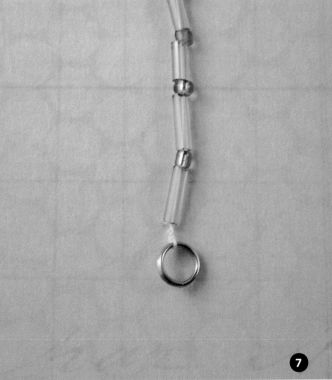

7

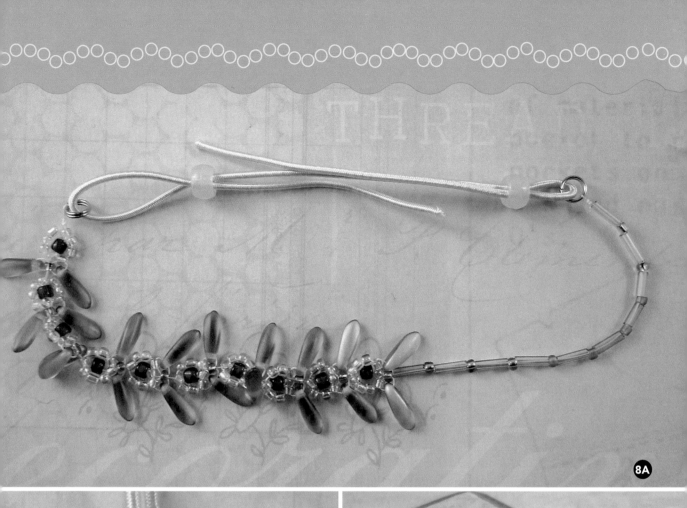

8A

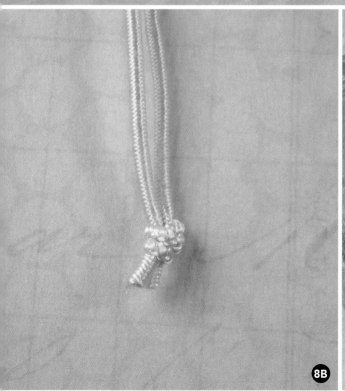

8B

Almost all of the supplies needed for the projects in this book can be found at your local craft store. Some items are one-of-a-kind or more difficult to find because they are not in high demand for craft stores to carry and can be purchased from online suppliers instead. Items like swivel hooks, hex nuts, parachute cord, coated telephone wire, and jute twine may be available at your local hardware store if you cannot find them at a craft store. More exclusive items used for projects in this book can be found through the following online retail sources.

Snowman head bead for the Snowman Zipper Pull
Cupboard Distributing
www.cdwood.com

Watch face for the Twirly Whirly Watch Bracelet
Fire Mountain Gems and Beads
www.firemountaingems.com

Night-light lamp shade frame kit for the Crystal Night-Light Shade
The Lamp Shop
www.lampshop.com

Dritz Fashion Buckle for the Macramé Skater Cuff
Jo-Ann Fabrics and Craft Stores
www.joann.com

About the Author

Amy Kopperude is an artist, graphic designer, and editor living in York, PA. She grew up in Minnesota among talented family members who supported her creative growth from an early age. Amy is an avid crafter who likes to dabble in all kinds of media and especially enjoys working with small, intricate pieces. She has been creating and designing with beads for many years and occasionally teaches beading workshops for kids and teens. She is also the author of *Bead Bugs: Cute, Creepy, and Quirky Projects to Make with Beads, Wire, and Fun Found Objects*.

INDEX

DON'T MISS THE OTHER BOOKS IN THE SERIES!

Creative Kids Complete Photo Guide to Crochet
Deborah Burger
ISBN: 978-1-58923-855-8

Creative Kids Complete Photo Guide to Sewing
Janith Bergeron and Christine Ecker
ISBN: 978-1-58923-823-7

MORE BOOKS ON BEADING

Bead Bugs
Amy Kopperude
ISBN: 978-1-58923-732-2

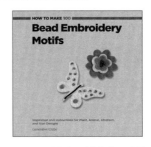

How to Make 100 Bead Embroidery Motifs
Geneviève Crabe
ISBN: 978-1-58923-779-7

The Complete Photo Guide to Beading
Robin Atkins
ISBN: 978-1-58923-718-6

Bead Jewelry 101
Ann and Karen Mitchell
ISBN: 978-1-58923-665-3